TRYHARD

TRYHARD

A Cautionary Tale of Clocking In and Spinning Out

LAURA MAYER

HARPERONE
An Imprint of HarperCollins*Publishers*

Photo of Betty Lehan Harragan on page 214 reproduced with permission of Kathleen Harragan Polutchko.

Quotes from *Games Mother Never Taught You.* Copyright © 1977 by Betty Lehan Harragan. Reprinted with permission by Kathleen Harragan Polutchko.

Quote by Fay Weldon reproduced with permission of Curtis Brown Group Ltd, London on behalf of The Estate of Fay Weldon. Copyright © Fay Weldon.

Quote from *The Old Farmer's Almanac.* Copyright © 2014 by Yankee Publishing Incorporated ISSN 0078-4516. Printed with permission of The Old Farmer's Almanac, 2015.

Quote from *The Bell Jar* by Sylvia Plath. Copyright © 1971 by Harper & Row, Publishers, Inc. Used by permission of HarperCollins Publishers.

Quote from *Tracy Flick Can't Win* by Tom Perrotta. Copyright © 2022 by Tom Perrotta. Reprinted with permission by Tom Perrotta.

hc.com

FIRST EDITION

Designed by Yvonne Chan

Library of Congress Cataloging-in-Publication Data has been applied for.

ISBN 978-0-06-338050-9

Printed in the United States of America

26 27 28 29 30 LBC 5 4 3 2 1

Author's Note

This is a work of nonfiction. The events and experiences detailed herein are all true and have been faithfully rendered as I have remembered them, to the best of my ability. Some names, identities, and circumstances have been changed in order to protect the integrity and/or privacy of the various individuals involved.

Though conversations come from my keen recollection of them, they are not written to represent word-for-word documentation; rather, I've retold them in a way that evokes the real feeling and meaning of what was said, in keeping with the true essence of the mood and spirit of the event.

Author's Note

To Joanna and Maureen

The country did not want cryhards or diehards: it wanted tryhards and workhards—and if they moved forward in that spirit, animated by that temper, free from all bitterness [. . .] they might hope [. . .] to accomplish something.

Sir Gordon Hewart, 1st Viscount Hewart,
quoted in *The Times* of London on January 21, 1922.
According to the *Oxford English Dictionary*, this is
the first printed use of the word "tryhard."

Contents

Contents

Introduction

I live to work. I believe I am not alone. I believe I am an extreme variation on a type. If you picked up this book, a book purposefully, luringly titled *Tryhard: A Cautionary Tale of Clocking In and Spinning Out*, my guess is we share this type. Moth to flame. We work to acquire the target, always slightly beyond reach. For me that's the stability of owning a home. For you, it could be something else, something less tangible. But you and me, we're clawing toward our targets together.

I am, as of this typing, an executive producer at a storied news organization you've likely heard of. I've been the producer behind many podcasts you've potentially listened to and many, many others you likely haven't. I've managed multimillion-dollar budgets. I've worked with celebrities. I was technically a record executive. I regularly speak onstage. I've been on television.

By almost any external measure, I've had success—in radio and, more successfully, in podcasting. An attainably successful career that could count as lightly aspirational to you, dear reader.

But if you ask me if I'm successful, I'll point you to the times I've made a fool of myself. Openly trying is, in and of itself, embarrassing. This book is a mid-lifetime of trying. I've done the trials to see the errors. And, as you'll read in this book, there are many errors. None of which will stop me from forging ahead to try to meet my goal.

Last year, to up my game, I invested in a Pavlok. The Pavlok company states that its electronic device, which looks like a first-generation Fitbit, is meant to help users break bad habits. My bad habit is sleeping too soundly. The Pavlok lives on my wrist and, at 5:30 a.m. every day, shoots 340 volts of electricity into my body. It feels like I'm being rhythmically burned by three cigarettes on my inner wrist. I use this instead of an alarm clock, which cannot compete with my REM, no matter how loud or bright it's set.

The Pavlok's burning shocks won't stop until I run out of my bed and to my refrigerator to scan a QR code. No mercy. My cats—Hector, Lulu, and Pruney—run alongside me, knowing that my bolting means soup's on. Recently I developed arm sores from the Pavlok's electrodes. This is not the Pavlok's fault. This is my body's fault because it cannot stop sleeping.

But I am a thirty-eight-year-old elder millennial who lives to work, so it is worth it.

My husband, Danny, and my daughter, Joanna, sleep on.

My aim, upon rising, is to clock work hours. But I am not a perfect person. I fritter away at least a half hour playing a time-management game wherein I serve cakes to a series of increasingly angry cartoon pixels. This game makes me actively angry. I get worked up. The game is basically a facsimile of a manic restaurant job. Every day I shock myself awake at 5:30 a.m. to work a stressful fake job before I start my stressful real job.

But that is not a contradiction for those who live to work. I think you understand.

Before I begin the work I am paid to do each morning—that is, to produce podcasts for a corporation you've likely heard of—I glue a miniaturized chandelier or carton of milk or strip of velvet wallpaper into my daughter's dollhouse. The dollhouse, which I researched for at least forty hours before purchase, is a stand-in for the house I cannot afford to give my family. It is a place to glue the *stable, material items* I can bear the cost of only in miniature, in pretend, because the real ones are still out of reach.

It is after all this—and a bit of parenting—that I finally look at my Apple Watch, which I wear on my left hand to avoid the Pavlok sores on my right, and realize that I am very, very late for work. I grab my bag and throw on my coat.

I run through the leafy streets in Ditmas Park, Brooklyn, hoping that my train will defy physics and make an hour trip in just twenty-five minutes.

I'm doing what I've always done: getting to where I want, faster than humanly possible.

There are drawbacks to this approach.

There are reasons for its extremity.

TRYHARD

Job 1

My First Job

In December 1996 there was a crackle in the air across the entirety of American suburbia. An excitable nervousness, primarily emanating from packs of prepubescent teen boys. That's a powerful, clammy mass to enliven. It was nearly Christmas, and every one of these spiritually undulating children wanted the same gift: the newly released Nintendo 64 game console.

I was feeling the crackle, the excitement, the anxiety, while standing with my mother in line at the recently erected Einstein Bros. Bagels in our small town. We rarely spent time together at all. Even though she was almost constantly at home, she was defiantly elsewhere from where I was, from where my brothers were. I hoped she was closing the distance over bagels.

Nine-year-old me made it out to be a ladies' lunch. I showered. I wore my best overalls. I made sure the car was warmed up before she got into it, to drive us to Einstein Bros. The warm crackle of the attention, finally, of my distant yet always present mother.

"You see that guy at the end? The one wrapping the sandwiches," she said.

"Yeah."

"He's got one long pinky nail. That's a coke nail."

"Coke?"

"Cocaine! Jesus," she said, grabbing the two sandwiches from Mr. Coke Nail. Noted.

I expected that she'd want to eat the sandwiches in her car, a black Nissan with fabric seats, the engine running to keep the heat on and to provide a quick escape if she saw someone she knew out the window. She didn't like to be out in public for reasons I didn't then understand. As I went for the store's door, she took the sandwiches to a table in the center of the restaurant. A table where we would sit together, alone, in public, for the first time that I could remember.

As we unwrapped our bagels, I could tell that something was off. Her hands weren't shaking, and her voice was loose—not slurring, but nearly. Her jaw floating rather than set.

In that moment I kicked myself. My calculations were wrong. She was drinking again, or she never stopped. I had let my hope get the better of what I knew, deep down, to be true.

The trajectory of an alcoholic is almost impossible to

chart. Trust me. I spent ten years trying to do it. I kept literal tabs on my mom's drinking by tracking its ups and downs, by day of the week, via a five-point scale, in what I called "The Chart." At the end of my day, I'd sit at my desk and track how drunk she seemed that day, with graph paper, a pencil, and a ruler, on a scale of 1 through 5.

Wednesday, less drinking, less screaming: 2.
Thursday, more drinking, more screaming: 4.
Friday, never stopped drinking, intense screaming: 5.
Etc.

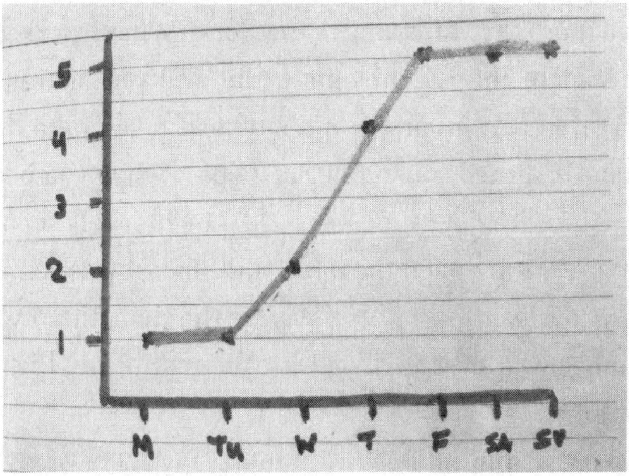

This is like the Saffir–Simpson scale, the hurricane-wind categorization system—a similarity you can dial up or down as you like. And, like a hurricane, Category 5 presents the most immediate danger. But Category 3 can still linger over a warm body of water for days and eventually wipe an entire town out when it makes landfall.

I'd concluded that Sundays were the worst days by far, as both my parents would've been drinking consistently for two days by then. By 3:00 p.m. on Sundays, they'd grown fed up with their situation, their families, themselves.

Prior to Coke Nail Bagel Lunch, there'd been a streak of Level 1 "A-okay" days, as I wrote them in The Chart, over the course of my two-week winter break. I took my mother's invitation to lunch as a sign that she was potentially moving through something. That she'd show up, both physically and presently, for me. This was what I always wanted. What I needed more than anything in the world. What I worked for.

As she ate the bagel sloppily, the drunken energy that would often turn to anger and rage had taken on a different tone. It turned conspiratorial. I guess when you begin a lunch date with your nine-year-old daughter talking about cocaine, any topic is on the table. And since it was so rare to sit together like this, I knew, even at the time, that I would remember whatever was said for the rest of my life. This transcended the rules of The Chart.

"We're getting him the Nintendo," my mom said, with disgust.

"Brian?" My twin brother, one of the prepubescent cracklers who'd been lobbying for an N64 since the fall. My older brother would also benefit from this acquisition.

"Yeah. He doesn't know it, so don't tell him."

"Okay, I won't. Why did you and Dad say he couldn't have it?"

"We can't afford it. He doesn't deserve it."

There was cream cheese all over her mouth and now on the sleeve of her sweater—and not a small amount, a full glop.

So, you're nine years old, sitting at a table in a bagel chain with your mom, who is drunk, and who will soon be driving. She's disheveled and angry at my twin brother for unknown reasons. He's getting the prize of Christmas 1996 but will be told he doesn't deserve it. You're excited to know a secret from your mother, someone who seems to trade exclusively in secrets. You're excited for your brother—and, let's be real, for yourself—for the N64. You've discovered the existence of something called cocaine having to do with long fingernails. Your graph of your mother's drinking needs new categorization for this type of drunken activity—this pseudo-friendship drunken outing. There's a lot of new data to incorporate.

Though, I could tell my mom was a regular-old Level 3 drunk by the time she finished eating. By then she was complaining about my dad in terms a daughter shouldn't hear. I was uncomfortable, but, at the same time, I felt that light from her, the attention. It was painful but it was there: the warm, rough, dirty coat suddenly put onto a freezing child.

I also knew, from when the police officers visited Girl Scout Troop 217, that you should never get into a car with a drunk driver. But what if that drunk driver is your mother? The police officer didn't cover that one. More calculations. This conversation, and many similar conversations like it, went something like this:

"Should we walk home? It's nice out," I asked.

"No, Laura, it's snowing."

"What if we went to the Starbucks?"

"No, I want to go home and watch TV."

"I have to . . . go to the library," I said.

"So, you're not going to get in the car with me, your mother who just bought you lunch and spent time with you?" she said, with disgust.

"No, I've got to go to the library to study."

"Ungrateful bitch."

I knew with that last remark she was at a Level 4. I watched her swerve away alone.

On that day, and on many others after, I made the decision to save myself over my mother's self. Or, that's how it felt. How it still sometimes feels.

It's no surprise that my adult work, as producer of radio and then podcasts, became trying to control the uncontrollable. Trying to predict situations as best I could before they happened. An interview prepped. A script written. A caller screened. Checking the literal and figurative temperature of a room. All of that work, my work now, started with The Chart, which required all of those same skills. Keeping The Chart, to try to predict and care for my mother in the ways she would tolerate, was my original job. And, damn, if it wasn't hard to quit.

And an unabashed tryhard was born.

* * *

I have read my fair share of business books. Your *#Girlbosses*, your *Leans Ins*, your executive-suite-or-bust manifestos. I gravitated toward them in my twenties, and they shaped my early thinking on career and identity. For a time, on this planet, no one was more invested in annual reviews, key-performance indicators, and "executive presence" than I was. The books in the genre spoke to my worldview and life plan: to inhabit a series of jobs that controlled the uncontrollable . . . forever.

Now, after approximately twenty-eight years of worship at the altar of workplace excellence, as I lurch into my late thirties, I'm interested in detangling the hornet's nest of misplaced motives that got me to this moment and helping others do the same.

This book is an assemblage of the jobs I've held and my relentless but always virtuous attempts to vanquish them. It is filled with lessons learned—and ignored—on the off chance you'll see one worth heeding.

* * *

The overall job I've inhabited most successfully and longest: professional podcast and radio producer.

When did I know I wanted to be a professional podcast and radio producer? Around sixth grade, when I began working at the Glencoe Public Library, where I spent so much time that, once I aged out of the summer reading contest (which I won five summers in a row), they offered me a job to keep me busy. It was there that I somehow learned about the radio program *This American Life* on WBEZ and became hooked.

If anyone asked, WBEZ was where I wanted to work. This answer remains constant, to some degree, today.

A photo from one of my summer reading championship wins. Taken by the dearly departed children's librarian Mrs. Hauser.

Why was a child so taken with public radio? A medium traditionally for the mid-to-upper-level age group, the intellectual commuter? The stories I heard on *This American Life* allowed me to escape to a version of adulthood that made sense to me. One different from the chaotic way my parents moved through their lives. Most of the stories had personable characters and a beginning, a middle, a surprise, and a tidy ending. What I most sought out in life.

I burned episodes of *This American Life* onto CDs and listened to them on my portable CD player while shelving books in the children's library. Barely older than the kids checking out the books, I felt like a spry ghost haunting those stacks. While shelving *S*'s for *Sachar, Scieszka, Smith,* I'd get to *Stine,* as in R. L., and think to myself: *Why would all these kids want to read scary stories of frightened children, just to become frightened children themselves?* Even then my imagination couldn't take that extra input. I had a live-action version at home. So, I self-soothed myself with radio stories of thirtysomethings finding small, funny bits of closure.

Good radio producers, I would learn in time, must always take the temperature of any room they're in. They must look around corners to plan for any potential problems that may cause the work to go awry.

For example, say you're booking an interview guest about presidential hair. To be ready for anything, you must listen to other interviews this guest has done on the topic, so your host doesn't lob questions already asked and answered. You must find out if this so-called presidential hair expert had a previous beat and how that old beat relates now. Is there any evidence—in online discourse, or via in-person gossip—that the host potentially hates this guest, or vice versa? And most bedeviling of all: voice! Is the guest a mumbler, a whisperer, a speed-talker who makes no sense? Will they be game for certain conversational detours or choke if taken off-road? Can you whack through the red tape of publicists and/or managers and get that guest on the phone before the booking for a test run?

Prep calls save producers' lives.

When I started making my own radio stories, I dutifully asked guests the standard "check the levels on the mic" question: What did you eat for breakfast? This to tease out possible sound and voice issues. As the years have gone by and I've gotten savvier, I've changed the prompt: "Tell me the story of when you've most embarrassed yourself at work." This accomplishes a few things: It elicits responses that cause the sound meters to really move (harsh intakes of breath, often a "Woo-boy"). It also catches interviewees off guard, forcing them to sink into themselves and give a better interview.

In these ways, I've been professionally training as a producer since I was conscious.

* * *

Smash cut to twenty-five years since cocaine nail–gate, and right now, at this very moment, I'm leaning over my kitchen countertop, late for work, and reading emails on my phone. Email parkour. I'm furious about getting uninvited from a meeting. So upset that the various biometric devices I wear (an Apple Watch and an Oura Ring) have pushed notifications to my phone to the effect of *You good?*

Joanna, my daughter, three and a half years old, looks on. "Mommy workin'," is what she says to Danny, my husband, as she returns to organizing papers into a stack on her tiny desk. Mommy is, indeed, working.

This meeting I'm fuming about is intended for everyone in the building who shares my title. It's part of a series of meetings having to do with larger network strategy. Since I began at this company, I've been invited and then uninvited from all the executive producer meetings—the only executive producer in the organization to hold this distinction. Yes, I am bragging.

How can I control the uncontrollable from the sidelines, I ask you?!

How can you, fellow tryhard?

My husband knows how easily agitated this sort of org-chart hijack can get me. I feel spiritually neutered. My therapist is hip to it, too. And my biometric recording devices sure as hell have me pegged. A more regulated person might not be so upset about getting uninvited from meetings, particularly in work cultures that are so dominated by them. But, when you're kept out of the loop, you're kept from doing the work you're trying with all your might to do.

In my defense, my agitation is quiet to the outside observer. Perhaps some light huffing and puffing. A scrunch of the nose and mouth, eyes turning to beads, like a squirrel eager for its next nut. Inside, I am on fire. But a slight isn't actually required to achieve this fire. If I'm being honest, this fire has been with me every day of my life.

||

Job 2

I Am the Executive

Willingness to serve is not enough; you must know how to do the job well, even in an emergency.

Girl Scout Handbook (1947 edition)

I met all of my friends, from second grade through high school, via the Girl Scouts. Girl Scout Troop 217, to be exact. Scouting was my first outside-of-home job. The other troop members were my first colleagues.

As I remember it, after the first half-day of second grade, the troop leaders held an informational meeting for aspiring Brownies in a recreation room attached to a bone-dry ice-skating rink. The only requirements? The willingness to work as a team and to pay two dollars a month for juice and crackers. The Scouts met weekly. We earned badges together. We cleaned up trash and went on nature walks. We earned badges separately. (I spent months working on my presentation to get the weather badge. It involved a poster board and securing signed photos of two of Chicago's local meteorologists. One of whom, Tom Skilling, has a brother, Jeffrey Skilling, who was deeply embroiled in the Enron scandal. I thank Tom Skilling for his generosity during that trying time.)

The Scouts' work anchored me. And the troop's leaders, the moms of my Scout friends, saved me. I glommed on to those moms (spiritually, if not physically—I'm not a hugger) when mine wasn't available.

In the most literal sense they fed, housed, and occasionally clothed me. They also put up with my early tryhard tendencies.

A scene from 1997: It's 7:30 a.m., and I'm ten years old. I have just walked upstairs to see my favorite sight: a mom sitting alone with a cup of coffee. It's just me and the Mom. She's a sitting duck with her Folgers, listening to one of those white laminate nineties kitchen TVs quietly in the background. She's not quite awake. But I am. And the Mom is not my mom. That is my favorite type of mom. The previous night was a sleepover. Likely I forced the group to work overtime on a particular badge procurement—probably having to do with recycling, because that's all I recall talking about in 1997—and it went long, and I slept in this poor, tired woman's finished basement with the rest of Troop 217.

I'm the first one to bed and the first one up. And, because of this, I get to do my second favorite thing after ruthlessly gobbling down the Bagel Bites she bought with her hard-earned money: I get a tête-à-tête with the Mom at her breakfast nook, whether she wants to or not.

When you're a kid who has been forced to grow up quickly, through traumatic or regular reasons, or because you were born with something that others call an "old soul," which simply means you seem tired and sad most of the time, you may have spent much of your childhood more comfortably talking with adults than with other kids. I was one of those kids—those adult wannabees, with an old soul and an intense nature—and Peggy, the Mom currently in my crosshairs, was familiar with my need to gab.

Peggy is wearing a purple housedress and a look of warmth as I bound toward her. An adult, all mine, in the early-morning hours! The bubbling freshness of my endless questions are meant to spark a rollicking conversation: "What's the weather like today?" "Do you know what the barometric pressure is?" "How often do you mow your lawn?" "How do you feel about Hillary Clinton?" "Has your hair always looked that way?" I've never been giddier. From my vantage, now, as a tired mom myself, the pressure was on for poor Peggy. How to entertain this bubbly pit of need?

But then Peggy asks a question I'll never forget: "Do you know what you said to everyone last night?"

Do I know what I said to everyone last night? No, Peggy, I do not. And now I am very quiet.

"You fell asleep before everyone else," Peggy says.

I know that. I am proud of that. What's your point, Peggy?

"And then you shot up and yelled 'I AM THE EXECUTIVE!'"

The horror starts sinking in.

"The girls came to get me to make sure you were okay. But we figured you were just sleep talking."

I am quiet after that. Which is probably what Peggy was aiming for. Check and mate, Peggy.

* * *

I can explain. Around the time I met the Scouts, in 1995, I started watching a lot of *Murphy Brown* while doing homework. The lead, Candice Bergen's character, became an obsession. An owner of a desk, at the center of a team, determined to rev up her career at a national television network after a personal and professional fall?! No man to depend on, no child (in the early seasons) to care for? Murphy was the epitome of power to my young brain.

I've recently rewatched the first episodes and now realize that the premise of the series is that Murphy Brown is a recovering alcoholic who has recently completed a stint in rehab and is trying to make her comeback in network news. Relevant to me on several levels today, sure. But I didn't put the pieces together then.

My interpretation of Murphy was as pure heroine. I'd

push my nana's old yellow desk to the center of my bedroom and force my twin brother to dictate memos, bring me things from other parts of the house (an orange, a hat, a calculator), and yell at the employee I/Murphy Brown despised. If I was met with any pushback, I'd remind my twin brother: "I am the executive!"

I brought this energy to the Girl Scouts. I brought it to Peggy's house. I leaked it in the middle of the night.

As I rewatch *Murphy Brown* now, I realize that her nemesis was, in fact, the executive producer of the show, Murphy Brown's boss. As, technically, an executive producer at a television network today, I have since become my own nemesis. But middle-age does that to us all, doesn't it?

Job 3

Tracy Flick

I wasn't the president. I wasn't even the principal of Green Meadow High School.

Tracy Flick, from Tom Perrotta's *Tracy Flick Can't Win*

Lesson: Never do a job half-assed, even if you've got half the resources everyone else has.

Throughout my childhood I was lucky to attend well-funded public schools full of high achievers. I was one of those kids who volunteered to read the morning announcements over the loudspeakers: My weather reports were a hit in fourth grade. My friends and I collected extracurricular activities like others collected Pokémon.

School became my second outside-the-house job.

When a friend of my brother's informed me in junior high that grades "don't matter" until high school, I remember thinking the boy needed his head examined.

As someone who was regularly reminded of her *permanent record*—as in, if I were to say anything about my parents to anyone it would result in my going to "military school" and ruin my "permanent record"—I understood the real game.

Junior high school became high school. The class of 120 kids who knew one another's names and parents and, often, home phone numbers by heart, suddenly became a class of one thousand students, many hell-bent on competing with one another for college placement from their first step into the school.

This achievement culture grew in lockstep with the wealth around me. My neighbors were rich and getting richer. They had pools, summer sleepaway camps, family vacations, circular driveways on which they could drive their SUVs in endless circles (why back up when you can just keep on driving forward?). They had ACT tutors, Land Rovers, and their very own braces. Oh how I envied their braces. I dreamed of attaching thick rubber bands to both sides of my upper and lower jaws and crying tears of joy every night.

The village where I grew up—Glencoe, Illinois—and the surrounding towns, were favorite settings for John Hughes, the writer and director who most accurately captured the wealth and ease of the northern Chicago suburbs in the 1980s. See: *The Breakfast Club, Home Alone, Ferris Bueller's Day Off, Sixteen Candles.*

The high school where *The Breakfast Club*'s five delinquents served their time? That's Glenbrook North High School, a school that my high school played in basketball. The famous *Home Alone* house? That was within spitting distance of my village's orthodontist. The house was recently sold for 5.5 million dollars. A true steal. The scene in *Ferris Bueller's Day Off* where Ferris and Sloane attempt to talk Cameron off a literal stone ledge when Cameron discovers the additional mileage he put on his dad's Ferrari? That was filmed at the Glencoe beach, just blocks from the library where I toiled in high school. The final scenes of *Sixteen Candles* were filmed at the Glencoe Union Church, whose shadow I was under while avoiding playing softball during the summers (most memorably, my Tamagotchi died while I was in the outfield on one of those hot days; I hope the Holy Ghost remains with the dearly departed).

The 2020 census ranked Glencoe as one of the top twenty wealthiest communities in the United States. My parents bought our house in 1984, before Glencoe became ritzy. You could hear the Metra commuter train from my bedroom, rolling at regular intervals into downtown Chicago. Just thinking of that rumble, the regularity, the sound of the horns as the safety gates lowered on Harbor Street, lowers my blood pressure.

Being so close to these kids' wealth and stability was confusing when I was younger.

"Aren't you the girl who ate all our food?" said a friend's

older brother to me, on installment two of two playdates, an Eggo waffle hanging halfway out of my mouth.

Yes, I was the girl who ate many—though, not all, I will say to this day—of their snacks at the first playdate. Because I was hungry and I didn't have a snack of my own.

This brief snack inquisition was the moment I realized that what they had was not mine. And, what I had wasn't theirs. But, in time, I learned there were ways to get what I wanted.

School. And. Work.

From the start of high school, I piled on the hardest classes and picked up extracurricular activities like my lint roller now picks up cat hair. I was on Peer Jury, the local snitch committee, where the Girl Scouts (now hormonal) and I sentenced our peers to community service for doing slightly illegal things. I volunteered for Safe Ride, working the phones in the basement of a church once a month, speaking to drunken kids leaving parties who needed a safe ride back home. Imagine the gossip! I founded the Claymation Club. I was the editor in chief of the yearbook. I wrote a weekly column for the newspaper. I was voted "Most Likely to Edit *The New York Times*," a job no one would ever or should ever give me. All of this was in an effort to, yes, strengthen my eventual college application but also to stay the hell away from the increasing instability of the Mayer lair.

I found creative ways to invent more time for all of it. I took early-bird classes that started at 6:30 a.m. I'd stand in a blizzard waiting for the 5:55 a.m. Pace Bus 213 in layers of clothing I'd outgrown and which my parents could not afford to replace, my arms sticking out slightly to the sides like a penguin, raised by the many layers of fabric.

And, often, I overcommitted and had to dig myself out of holes.

Like that C- in freshman honors English.

It didn't seem to matter that I read every book twice. That I finished my papers ahead of time. My gritted-teeth effort was getting me nowhere. I was reading *The Odyssey* for class—the Sirens!—when my teacher, Mr. Pariano, took me aside and informed me that I needed to transfer down a level, that I wasn't qualified for his class.

I immediately set an appointment with the dean of the freshman campus. When I arrived at his office, he was surprised my parents weren't with me. Apparently, it's usually the parents who spearhead the appeal process.

"Dropping a class level isn't a failure," he said.

I looked at him, dead-eyed. My expectations of myself were zero sum: I was either doing things well or I was a failure.

Or in the inimitable words of Tracy Flick from Tom Perrotta's *Election*, "This country was built by people just like me who work very hard and don't have everything handed to them on a silver spoon. Not like some rich kids who everybody likes because their fathers own Metzler's Cement and give them trucks on their sixteenth birthday . . ."

I asked if there was anything I could do to stay in honors English. We settled on a probationary period. If I could raise my grade by the end of the semester, I could stay.

Don't tempt me with a good time.

The next English assignment in that honors class I was not leaving to chance: the personal essay. "And I don't want to read any essays about your grandparents," Mr. Pariano told us.

I wrote an essay about seeing my dad cry—for the first and only time—when our dog, Bob, died. Mr. Pariano read my essay aloud to each of his English classes. At the end of reading it during my class he said, "I think we have a writer in here."

So, you can, in part, blame Mr. Pariano for this book. Mr. Pariano, thank you for your encouragement. I hope you bought this book at full cost and in hardcover to further support my future as a writer.

There was no way I was going to let myself and my shortcomings stand in the way of trying my absolutely pathological hardest to get the best grades I possibly could. I gave myself full permission to sink into my full-bodied intensity in the name of my own achievement. I still give myself that permission.

During finals week I somehow turned it up a notch. Classes were canceled, and students were meant to use that time to study as hard as possible for their final exams. Most of my friends would get together to study—sit at the local

Caribou Coffee and read in comfortable silence, taking notes and regular breaks. But my system of rote memorization required too much table space and revealed too much of my secret scaffolding, to make studying a social event. I don't remember anything I learned in high school in part because I learned everything by copying all the words and theories and formulas onto note cards. I would sit and force my then-elastic brain to remember all of these things—threatening my mind, really, to grab on. I'd carry those forced facts, from the initial memorization through the final exam, and then empty them out afterward while watching *Laguna Beach* or drinking a Chantico (a thick hot chocolate SKU briefly offered by Starbucks in the early aughts).

If this early effort impresses you, reader, and you are in a position to hire me, I can be reached at laura@lrm.works. I am presently employed but never closed off to opportunities. And I mean never.

But, more on point, I look back at my time at New Trier Township High School fondly. Despite my scholarship as self-flagellation, that school gave me purpose and, eventually, direction—away from my crumbling family situation and toward something new.

||||

Job 4

Reinvention

But her life was just now full of hope and action: she was not only thinking of her plans, but getting down learned books from the library and reading many things hastily.

George Eliot, *Middlemarch*

Reinvention is an important job skill. You do not want the position you're currently in forever, am I right? Let me elucidate.

In *Felicity*, the show I obsessed over in high school, the main character, Felicity Elizabeth Porter, played by Keri Russell, transforms herself from an invisible high school tryhard to a stunning college coed with a fearless and unshakable will. She forms the crush that propels her after holding a bag of a boy's blood during her sophomore year of high school (it was a blood drive, but still). In the pilot episode she informs her parents that she would not be attending Stanford University, near her parents' home in California, and instead is going to a less-prestigious school across the country. She craved both the boy whose blood she held in high school and, at her core, a break from her controlling, high-achieving parents. In response her parents refused to pay tuition.

At college, she works two jobs—one, a work-study gig, where she filed (and at one point illicitly peeped at) paper copies of students' admission applications; a second as a barista at a TV version of Dean & Deluca, the famous fancy NYC grocer. When not surveilling or butting herself into her friends' business, she flirts with two bewildered boys and spends the rest of her time looking beautiful while serenely studying in her bed (next to a landline telephone). I connected to Felicity's quiet, semi-horrifying intensity.

I wanted in. Reinvention was my new job.

I asked my parents if I could apply to New York University, the school most closely resembling the fictional college that Felicity attends. They said, "No, and good luck paying for it if you do get in." Unlike Felicity, I compromised.

My father went to Northwestern University in the 1970s, a school twenty minutes from where I grew up. A prestigious school! Because I studied and worked in high school like my life depended on it, I figured I had a chance of getting into Northwestern. I calculated that they'd be more understanding of this plan. When I asked if I could apply to Northwestern University, they said, "You can, but good luck paying for it if you even get in."

My parents laughed at attending the school's prospective student tour, so I went with my friend Kam and her mother. We sat in a lecture hall to hear about the countless doors that a very expensive liberal arts education would open. I snuck toward the financial aid table and surreptitiously grabbed an information packet—noting I was the only kid in the room picking up those particular brochures. We then toured the campus with a spritely sophomore whose skills at walking backward and pointing I still remember to this day. I will say Northwestern University uses Lake Michigan—the greatest of the Great Lakes, and I will fight you on this—to its full advantage. Much of the campus's buildings sit on its coast—its blue water sparkling from every east-facing window. The architecture gave old, smart, and rich vibes—all adjectives I hoped to one day use to describe myself. Plus, the dorms. Oh, the dorms. A room of one's own with a twin extra-long bed, in which I wouldn't need to worry about whatever chaos was about to descend upon me from my parents, who would not live there. I pictured myself studying wistfully next to the recently defunct landline hookup, just like Felicity Porter. I'd wear sweaters and innocently bumble into other people's business in the same ways I saw Felicity doing. Like Felicity, it was the farthest I'd be able to get away in order to break from my family, despite only being seven miles away. I could feel myself at this school, on this campus, becoming a different version of myself.

The three of us—Kam, her mom, and I—got hot chocolate after the tour and debriefed. Kam didn't really want to go to Northwestern. To the rest of Girl Scout Troop 217, Northwestern was a "safety school." They would apply, sure, but matriculation would be a worst-case scenario. Going to Northwestern meant that you had not gained acceptance to any of the Ivy League schools. Meanwhile, I wanted in more than ever.

I met with my assigned college counselor that fateful summer and laid out my plan. He said that if I applied early decision my chances of getting admitted were higher. *Early decision.* No two words had ever sounded so good together. Looking back, I think he could sense my desperation, that this was more than your run-of-the-mill overachieving.

As *Felicity* summer turned into senior-year fall, I polished my personal essay, which detailed my first memory: being baptized in a bathtub by my great-aunt, who was a nun. No one read my essay except for me. I have a potentially false memory of sealing all of my admission materials in a large envelope and sending them to the school. I wonder how I figured out the postage. More likely, I probably applied online.

Early-decision decisions came out right around winter break. The day before the break, my college counselor came to find me in my first-period class: PE. The unit was "mindfulness," and all the students were lying on mats and listening to spa music, "watching" their thoughts and trying not to sleep. I was roused by the gym teacher and asked to come into the hallway.

The college counselor said, simply, "I got a good call," smiled, and left.

The official word arrived the following morning. Then I calmly ate a bowl of Lucky Charms and walked to my shift at the children's library.

My parents weren't around when I got the news. And, if they had been, I wouldn't have told them. Whatever was said—positive or negative—would've stuck to me. And now that I knew which direction I was headed, I wanted to scrape as much of their influence off me as possible.

Though, as I tiptoed across the icy sidewalks on my walk to the library, I started second-guessing myself. The family mantra of "Who do [I] think [I am]" to do, well, anything demanding or ambitious kept sneaking into my icily clear mind. As I peeled off my parka and many sweaters during my walk up the carpeted steps to the library's children's section, I wondered if I could even remain as driven without the threat of "Who do you think you are?" Was I making a mistake, with what I considered to be a hard break from my family? I believe this is called cognitive dissonance. The cusp of reinvention is a shock.

When I told the news to Mrs. Hauser, the librarian, she

hugged me so hard I thought my shoulders would dislocate. It didn't help that, when hugged, I have a tendency to pin my arms to my sides. She had tears in her eyes and said that "now is the time to do whatever you dream." I went to the cart of children's books, fired up my CD headset, and got to work putting away the books left over from the day before.

Somehow, word spread, and the members of Girl Scout Troop 217 showed up at the library to congratulate me. Most of them had also applied early decision and had gotten into their top-choice schools: Harvard, Yale, Brown, Penn. Ivy League schools. Northwestern was a cute choice, a safety school. For me it represented safety, full stop.

High school graduation was like a wedding for twelve hundred kids. The boys wore rented tuxedos. The girls wore long white gowns. My date for the reception that followed was the head of both the math team and the Scholastic Bowl. I didn't drink a drop of alcohol—and wouldn't until college. A longtime tradition for New Trier graduates is to stay up until the morning and watch the sunrise from the beach, overlooking Lake Michigan. The only photo I have from that night features me looking tired. The caption "I have a newborn, please leave me alone" would fit this image. I got home, took a nap, and was jostled awake hours later by my semi-drunk mother.

"So, what'd you do last night, Laura?"

"I graduated from high school."

"No, but what did you *do*?" she continued.

"We went to the Dunkin/Robbins and got coffee and ice cream at four a.m."

The answer was disappointing to her. She left my room, and I got ready to go to my next shift at the library.

On the night before I left for Northwestern my parents both got Level 5 drunk. I was going back and forth from my room to my dad's car to load up all the items for my dorm. At one point, after coming back in from the humid September heat, my parents cornered me in the entryway. I don't know if I slipped or if I was pushed, but suddenly both of my parents were standing over me, screaming. "Who are you to go to this school, Laura?" "Who do you think you are?" "You're going to fail. You're not going to make it." "You've made a big mistake."

It's hard for me to remember the details of the hard verbal and light physical abuse that night. On the fight, flight, freeze continuum, I was cold as ice. At some point they left. I stood up. I continued packing the car. I went back and forth in the thick air, sweating and focusing on my reinvention.

The next day was like every day after my parents got drunk and violent: It was like it never happened.

In the morning, my dad and I made the twenty-minute drive to Northwestern. The student welcome wagon took my carefully packed storage containers onto dollies, and I walked with them, and my dad, to my dorm room. I ended up in a single dorm room, which sounds like a dream, but this particular dorm—the Foster-Walker Complex (there's a band named after it)—wasn't my, or perhaps anybody's, first choice. I had turned in my medical forms late and got my last pick of the dormitories. My dad stood next to me and my containers, in my room with a lofted twin bed, a desk, and a small, rented refrigerator, and said, "I'll be in the car."

I listened as other people unpacked their belongings with their moms, music blaring from laptops, telling stories, all with their doors open. I shut my door and quickly unpacked my toothbrush and computer: two essentials I knew I'd need to find sooner rather than later.

I went downstairs to my dad, who was waiting in the car. "Let's take a walk," he said, suddenly nostalgic for his own time at Northwestern.

We crossed the street to South Campus. The campus was idyllic, the previous humid night turning into a crisp autumn morning.

My dad suggested going into the library. "I want to see if it has changed."

We walked in, and I saw the rows and rows of desks, the private study carrels, and the comfort of the books all around me. Since it was freshman move-in day, many of the librarians had set up little displays on tables, trying to lure in work-study students. I went up to a woman with long gray hair—younger than Ms. Hauser, but she certainly could have served as her stand-in for a stunt in an action movie—and asked about her department.

Her name was Carol Anthony. She ran the Mitchell

Multimedia Center at Northwestern. I asked her what happened at that center as my dad paged through a pamphlet. The gist: It's the place where students checked out and occasionally watched DVDs and laser discs.

Would I want to work there? she asked.

Suddenly I had a job.

I kept that job at the Multimedia Center for four school years and three summers. It quickly became clear that this was one of the most sought-after work-study jobs. You didn't really have to do much reshelving, and it was appropriate to watch movies when it was quiet.

I once asked Carol why I got the job. She said I was this meek little mouse with her dad, and she felt for me. During my freshman year I quickly developed a crush on a fellow Multimedia Center worker. During my sophomore year we suddenly ended up working all of our shifts together. It turns out, he went to Carol and asked to work with me because he had a crush on me, too. So Carol set me up not only with my first job in college but also with my college boyfriend. Carol also became my work reference for my first professional job. Later, after I'd been hired, that boss would come to my desk and say, "Boy, that librarian really likes you."

My dad left. I went back to my dorm room and cracked open the door to my new existence. I made my bed. Put away my many Felicity-inspired sweaters. Set up my very own laptop computer on the desk, which I paid for with my library earnings. The other parents slowly started leaving. Before my dad had left he gave me a carton of milk. "You'll need it."

I do drink one glass of milk a day, like Richard Nixon.

I started crying after he left. While I was lying sideways on the carpet of my new room, clutching my half gallon of milk, underneath the lofted bed where my mini-refrigerator sat, the enormity of the moment hit me. Who was I to have my own computer? Who was I to go to this expensive school, loans and scholarships aside?

Who was I?

In *Felicity* the pilot opens with Felicity talking to a tape recorder. She's recording an audio letter to her ex–French tutor and friend Sally Reardon (voiced by Janeane Garofalo). "I've never been able to talk to anyone like I can talk to her," she tells a friend in that first episode. "So instead of writing, I talk to her. And she talks back to me."

The audio monologues serve as both a clever narrative device for the series—Felicity has the ability to reveal what she's thinking when she, especially in earlier seasons, keeps her own wants and needs close. Of course, as an aspiring "radio person" I liked the whole idea of the voice recordings.

While lying on the carpet in my dorm room, on the first day of college, at the place I determined would be my escape from sadness, in the shaky beginnings of a reinvention that would lead me to a new me—I wished I had a Sally.

卌

Job 5

Internification

Nothing but ambition, nothing but the desire to get on, that's all there is in his soul.

Leo Tolstoy, *Anna Karenina*

Regular people get to ease into new jobs, tell themselves they can't learn it all on day one, that with time and immersion, they'll eventually do fine; tryhards assume they are behind upon arrival and never forgive themselves for it. It's jet fuel for the rest of their tenure.

Upon arriving at Northwestern's Medill School of Journalism, I determined that I was nowhere near ready to find the job that college was meant to secure me. And without that job, I could not sever my reliance on an unreliable home.

So instead of relishing the cushy four-year holding tank of academia, I turned all my attention to internships, the waiting rooms of the professional world.

The first internship, my freshman year, was at a television trade publication called something like *Television Sets Today*.

I referred to my boss as Mailer Daemon, an homage to the automated message you get when an email is undeliverable. He was the editor in chief. I watched him play the virtual world simulator *Second Life* on his desktop computer during most of my shifts. My duties required the normal intern fare: finding toner for the printer, acquiring coffee, sure. But I also wrote a series of blog posts for their website about the upcoming switch from analog to digital television broadcasting, which *Television Sets Today* was particularly on top of for very obvious reasons. It was 2006, just three years before the big switch from analog to digital mandated by the Federal Communications Commission, brought on by a need to free up signals for more television and radio broadcasts and the money that selling them would generate. This switch also (much later) ended up clearing the way for 5G cell service, which is how you're probably watching Netflix on the train to work and also somehow plays into how self-driving cars work. I didn't, and still don't, understand anything about this topic. Regardless, this meant that *Television Sets Today* was flush with advertisements for digital televisions—perhaps allowing Mailer Daemon a little more wiggle room to tend to his other life in *Second Life*.

One morning I came into the office and everyone was crowded around Mailer Daemon's empty desk. Mailer Daemon's deputy, who I'll call Emily, was hungover and covered in glitter. She looked panicked.

"I think we went out of business," she said casually. She then lit a cigarette inside the office.

"So what do we do?" I asked.

"Well, we have all this champagne. So we could drink that. But we should probably wait."

And wait we did. What exactly were we waiting for? Mailer Daemon to blast through the door, a briefcase of cash in hand, saving the magazine while neglecting his virtual family for the day? It wasn't clear to me why everyone thought the magazine was going out of business, but by the end of the day the staff members had started wheeling out furniture to their apartments.

"Go ahead, take a desk," Emily said, clearly having dipped into the champagne.

I left the office and took the long walk to the Loop, where I caught a commuter train that brought me back to Evanston. I did not take any office furniture. I didn't hear from anyone at *Television Sets Today* again.

Undeterred, I looked for another internship. I recalled the day that one of my journalism professors told a class full of freshmen, "Raise your hand if you've heard of blogs."

The equivalent today would be a professor asking a group of eighteen-year-olds if they knew about YouTube.

Nearly everyone in the audience raised a hand. Because, duh, if you ended up in journalism school in 2005, you were probably as online as someone could be in 2005, and the only thing to do was to read (and write . . .) blogs.

"Blogs are the future," the professor said without an ounce of self-consciousness.

I remember thinking, *Yes, and also the present and recent past.* And *Note to self: Do not go to college to find out about current events.*

Regardless, blog internships were my next pursuit. Which led me to *Gapers Block*. The blog covered arts, food, music, politics, sports, and local news in Chicago. I'd started reading it when it launched in 2003. Surely that gave me an edge. I sent a cold email to the editor in chief, asking if I could contribute. He said sure. I pressed for more details: a topic, a deadline, a length? I don't remember what he said. But I wrote an article and turned it in on time, which set me apart from some other *Gapers Block* contributors. (I type this now as I'm on my third extension for this very book.)

The editor in chief received my article and replied, "You should stop by sometime."

I took it upon myself to google his office location and show up, unannounced, the next day. The editor in chief seemed surprised but gamely brought me in and showed me around the company's coworking space. He asked me what I wanted to do when I grew up. I told him I was voted "Most Likely to Edit *The New York Times*." He smiled, then, paternally, invited me to drinks with the entire staff the following Friday.

At this point in my life I had started drinking but not in a serious way. When I got dragged to football games I would nurse a Jell-O shot and fall asleep, only waking up to the disgusting tradition of Northwestern football fans shaking their car keys whenever we played state schools. (I guess to suggest that Northwestern students had better cars than their opponents? I still cannot drive.) Sure, I'd puked at fraternities a few times, demurely, and significantly less than my counterparts. But it wasn't part of my life, yet.

This is all to say, I was not quite socialized enough to join a casual-drinks outing with people in their mid-to-late twenties. I was a little cat, weaned too early from her mother, sniffing around for something but not quite knowing what. This unfitness for polite adult society didn't stop me from taking the Red Line out to the Edgewater neighborhood of Chicago and showing up to watch these adults drink and chat.

I should also say that I looked about twelve years old at this time (and for about fifteen years after, including in my wedding photos). So a child strolls into a bar. The *Gapers Block* writers were confused. This child had many questions about their lives: "How did your begin your career?" "Did you do internships?" "How did you afford to do internships?" And some more invasive ones: "How much money do you pay for your rent?" "How much money did you make last week?" "Did you know you can sell pictures of your feet on the internet for money?"

Everyone was nice. But everyone hesitated before answering. Do you give a child answers to these questions? I left after an hour, citing an early start time at my university library shift. The front door of the pub practically blew open with their sighs of relief.

I had procured what mattered: my second internship!

Meanwhile, my studies were . . . not abandoned but deliberately neglected. I wrote every paper the night before it was due. The only book I remember reading in full was Bram Stoker's *Dracula* in a caffeine-fueled haze at a local coffee shop. I took my journalism classes more seriously—ever fearful of the "Medill F," which meant making a factual error and automatically failing the project—but I still earned many B's and C+'s. Despite fighting for every last point during high school, I did feel a transformation: I wanted and needed a job after college; I determined grades weren't going to get me there. I was trying to dump the present and move in with the future, whatever that might be. That last part is what I still wrestle with today. What tryhards the world over wrestle with.

There were other internships in Chicago onto which I threw my heavy determination. There were also many internships I applied for and did not get. To name a few: I failed the editing test for the *Chicago Reader* (the then-editor in chief's cell number is still in my phone). I didn't get two internships at WBEZ in Chicago but was accepted on my third go-around my senior year. I went in for an interview at the alternative weekly *Newcity*, getting there via the Metra train and then a treacherous walk along the highway. I arrived in full Tracy Flick mode—wielding a folder of my "clips," of every article I'd written for my internships and, probably, college assignments. I was wearing a tweed skirt suit in the middle of summer. Nowadays, someone would say my face looked "dewy," but I remember a bead of sweat dripping off my nose onto my upper lip during the interview with the incredibly laid-back deputy editor who managed the internships. He was wearing a T-shirt and had a wind-blown expression on his face upon meeting me. I followed up via email directly after the interview. I heard nothing back. I followed up the next day. (Pro tip: There's a big difference between "following up" and "hounding." I was hounding like a Westminster dog.) This time I got a response: I wasn't "the right fit."

The refrain to college students is "Enjoy it; this is the best time in your life." "The world," people say, "is your oyster."

Meanwhile, I was sweating in a tweed skirt suit on the side of the highway trying to force the future to come to me as quickly as possible. Lost, because I didn't have a smart phone. I was literally directionless.

I look back at college me tenderly, maternally. (My preschool-age daughter is closer to college than I am.) I'd advise that young me to slow down, to sit with that internal drive because it's central to her. To worry less about accomplishments and more about making mistakes and learning from them. I'd tell her to figure out what's fun, what her interests are apart from barreling forward.

At that age, we're all mysteries to ourselves and to others. Malleable by definition—hell, your frontal lobe isn't fully cooked until twenty-five. Relationships form quickly—and can last for the rest of your lives, or dissolve as fast as they started. I'd tell college me to get a slightly deforming haircut and watch it grow out. Because it doesn't matter! Enjoy the uncertainty because, and I hate this phrase that people tell middle-aged me now, "it will all work out in the end." But who likes uncertainty?

Finally, at the beginning of senior year, I was twenty-one and on my way to New York City—for the mother of all unpaid gigs: journalism residency.

A big draw for applicants to Northwestern's Medill School of Journalism was this mandatory quarter "abroad" program—at a magazine, newspaper, radio, or TV operation. It gives journalism students a chance to immerse in a future trade. And, luckily for me, it came with a housing stipend, while my loans and scholarships paid for my expenses.

Of course I wanted to work for the kind of organization that the school wasn't aware of yet. The conversation with my advisory professor went like this:

"I want to do podcasting,"

"Like, radio?"

"No, podcasts are different."

"Like, radio on the internet?"

"Sure."

Amazingly, he reached out to every news organization with a website—which, in 2008 was not as wide of a net as you'd expect—and asked if they did this thing called "podcasting." One publication did and had space for an intern: *Time* magazine.

I started work at the Time & Life Building on Monday, September 15, 2008. I arrived an hour early for my 10:00 a.m. meetup with my supervisor. I found a bench outside the building to kill some time and avoid arriving too early (by then I'd learned that showing up jarringly early tended to unnerve people) and to marvel at the turbocharged pace of the city, the creative ways people held takeout coffee, purses, and umbrellas with only two hands, and the tall shiny buildings that made downtown Chicago look like it was made out of LEGO bricks. Fast, fast, fast was what I wanted, and here I was, not just close to it, but *in it.* I sat still, for maybe the first time in my life, and thought about how I was the farthest away I'd ever been to anyone I was related to. I'd escaped! I sat with that feeling of finally being a different version of myself, a person released from the "Who do you think you are?" refrain from my childhood. I had made it to New York City, in the fall even (*Felicity* always felt very autumnal to me), to work in my chosen field: podcasts.

I watched workers enter the building on Fifty-First Street

ready to go to their desks, women click and clacking in high heels. People walked faster in New York, and I wondered what impact it had on their calves. I watched the revolving doors swish people in and spit people out. Increasingly, I noticed a few sad men wearing ties and holding white boxes. That seemed odd. Suddenly, there were many sad men, many white boxes, many ties flipped over shoulders. Turns out Lehman Brothers occupied several floors of the Time & Life Building, and that was the day the bank collapsed. Welcome to New York City and the Great Recession, baby!

At 10:00 a.m. I rushed in to meet Caitlin, my supervisor, and immediately decided she was the model of human I'd been looking to shape myself into. She seemed to hold a lot of power in every conversation she had. She was funny and down-to-earth, the latter being a quality I hadn't found much of at Northwestern. She also went to journalism school in the Midwest. She'd been at *The Washington Post* before *Time*. She was Canadian—how exotic! She spearheaded podcasting on Time.com and was happy to turn over as much of it to me as I wanted.

I got up every morning when I was in New York thrilled to be there. I indulged in my latent hereditary Catholicism and prayed every day that I would be able to make the city and this job be the setting for the rest of my life. I sensed, even then, that I was taking the business of landing work more seriously than my classmates were, many of whom didn't have the sudden appearance of the Holy Ghost to underscore their grasping. They were dealing with the sudden appearance of tube tops, of the possibility of dating finance-bro interns who would, soon, turn into actual finance bros.

In my spare time in New York, between the hours of 7:00 p.m. and 10:00 p.m. and on the weekends—I started an audio blog. I called it *Audio Everyday*. Every night, I'd record an episode about whatever happened to be on my mind that day: the Doppler effect; the original opening to the show *20/20*; Obama's promise to get his daughters a puppy upon winning the presidency. I'd post the little audio file to my blog and then watch an episode of *Gossip Girl*. The creative director of the Third Coast International Audio Festival, then a part of WBEZ Chicago, came across my audio blog. The little snippets about the majesty of Barbara Walters I lofted into the internet ended up being the reason I was finally (after the two failed attempts) accepted as an intern at WBEZ later that year.

In the morning I'd determinedly walk from my sublet in Hell's Kitchen to the *Time* offices in Midtown East, casing the sidewalks for my radio idols (as if I actually knew what they looked like). I showed up early to the office and stayed late. On nights and weekends, while my fellow classmates reported bacchanalian adventures, I returned to my lair, to my air mattress, to work on my audio blog and think about applying for more internships.

There was a lot of news going on at the time, so working in a newsroom was fairly lively. The Great Recession. Barack

Obama versus John McCain for president. As I got more comfortable at the job, more up in everyone's business, I asked if I could take over the duty of updating Time.com's Arts and Culture vertical.

"Sure," Caitlin, or someone else, must have said. It was not sought-after work. Updating the vertical required receiving a series of quotes and preselected images—original or from the newswire—going into a clunky software system, placing the stories with the corresponding images, copying and pasting some HTML tags, making sure nothing was wildly messed up, and pressing Publish. As I recall, the Arts and Culture vertical was updated a few times a day.

One day, right before lunch, I carefully updated the Arts and Culture vertical as usual, and pressed Publish. I took the elevators to this subterranean area of the building to Subway and bought a five-dollar Footlong (lunch and dinner). When I returned to my desk, I felt the clammy weight of many eyes on me.

"Laura, something happened," I recalled Caitlin saying. She sent me a link to *Gawker* (RIP), then the foremost site for media gossip.

I began reading:

"Is there any particular reason that *Time* magazine has a story (?) on its website right now with the byline 'By Ashley Alexandra Dupre'?"

I'll stop here for some explanation. In addition to all the national and world events unfolding in 2008, the previous spring *The New York Times* broke the story that New York's governor, Eliot Spitzer, was a frequent client of a high-priced escort service, to which he paid tens of thousands of dollars. Ashley Alexandra Dupre soon thereafter revealed her identity to the *Times* as one of the escorts. A media firestorm ensued that spring, which kept burning into the fall of 2008.

Gawker continued:

"The entire content of the story is a big picture of Ashley Alexandra Dupre, and the words 'I'm sorry for your pain.' Either the Spitzer hooker has been hired to write Zen koans, or something seriously strange is going on in *Time*'s internet department. "

It was me. I was the "something seriously strange" going on in *Time*'s internet department. And that item was definitely not supposed to be posted as a story.

While I was selecting the vegetables on my five-dollar Footlong, *Time* offered a comment to *Gawker*:

"(Now *Time* tells us this was supposed to be a 'Quote of the Day' that was accidentally converted into an article page. Crazy!) Click through for a big picture of the screen, in case it gets pulled."

What I was trying to post was a newswire photo of Dupre, with her quote "I'm sorry for your pain," within a "Quote of the Day" box on the Time.com Arts and Culture section. The tiny box was meant to sit quietly, in the upper-right-hand corner of the webpage, serving as a small flourish to the side of the actual stories on Time.com.

By the time I'd returned to my desk the article had indeed gotten pulled. An editor more senior than Caitlin beckoned me to her desk and said this was "bad" and asked if I knew about *Gawker*. Did I know about *Gawker*? Yes. I read *Gawker* at the university library's Multimedia Center desk during every shift, reveling in small-time media gossip about people I'd never meet, thinking about what it must be like to live in the snake pit of New York media. (But perhaps just to the side of the snake pit?) Yes, yes, I knew about *Gawker*.

"Can we, like, delete the internet?" I asked.

"No, that's not how the internet works," she responded.

She then started telling me about RSS feeds—basically an automated process that distributes articles and media.

"Oh!" I said, too happy-go-lucky for what the situation warranted. "Yes. Podcasts are published via RSS feeds."

"Okay, well," she continued, "that's part of the reason why you can't delete the internet." Once media is published on an RSS feed, it's sent out to anyone subscribed to that feed. Thousands, maybe millions, of people had copies, on their computers and phones, of my mistake. Plus, *Gawker* published a screenshot, so that was definitely that. The call girl's Zen koan was now part of my permanent record.

I returned to my desk blushed by embarrassment but not bright red. Sure, I'd made mistakes in my life at that point. Certainly more than I ever knew. But I had never gotten "into trouble" for anything in a school or work environment. I was told to be more careful next time. I pledged I would be careful. But something about making this unplanned mistake, which I look back on with more horror than I ever felt at the time, knocked something loose in me. So careful and particular, I remember this public mistake, and my ability to withstand it, as an actual before and after. I could withstand an honest-to-God fuckup and continue forward, red cheeks and beading sweat aside. I finally dropped perfection in favor of die-hard persistence. Ah, reinvention, at last.

卌 |

Job 6

Getting Started

Something will happen sometime soon.

A tattoo on my back

A tryhard never forgets her first Real Job.

The day after college graduation, which I did not attend, I got on an airplane alone to move to New York, for an internship at WNYC, New York Public Radio, which I could not afford.

This was not a real job, and I knew it. I got the internship via a cold email. (I later discovered I beat out Sigourney Weaver's niece for the position!) I funded this move to New York City through my college jobs at the university library, a pool of emergency funds that would last only until November.

That summer at WNYC, a very famous musician/DJ (his most famous album is called something like *Amusement*, and its songs still appear in commercials; the king of syncs!) approached nearly every female intern and young producer at the station and gave them his business card. The business card was a small piece of printer paper displaying his mononym, with an EarthLink email address. I, potentially fortunately, didn't receive an email invitation.

Rod Blagojevich visited the station for an appearance. In August 2009 the crooked Illinois governor who tried to sell Barack Obama's senate seat to the highest bidder was passing through New York to defend himself on as many media outlets as would have him. I do not remember where I was when he visited the station, but I remember the unsanctioned video/hit piece of Rod adjusting his hairpiece before his WNYC radio interview, which somehow got distributed to a political blog.

A series of people at WNYC got blamed for the leak and fired. And it looked, for a moment, like I was going to get my first radio job because of Rod Blagojevich's hair.

But while I was waiting twenty-four hours for the dust to settle after many of my work friends were fired, an assistant producer for a show called *Fishko Files*—a culture series that aired on WNYC and on NPR's *Morning Edition*, hosted by Sara Fishko—suddenly quit. Like Beetlejuice, my name was called three times, and I was there to assume the temporary (paid!) role of assistant producer. The only things the departing producer told me during his debrief was that he quit without another job lined up, and he suggested I find some good blogs to read since I'd have some time on my hands, because, he said, there wasn't much work to do in this position. And there was no possibility for advancement.

Had I been in a different phase of life, I might have heard this as a warning. But I needed a job. Few of my decisions made logical sense then, even the gambit of moving to New York in the first place. I was searching for direction without a compass.

During this time, I redirected my energy toward dating. I hung around with people I sort of knew from college, boys with theater degrees who drank beer, most of whom weren't working for pay and weren't too hung up on that detail. I wouldn't say I had a dating life more than I had a "try to convince people to date me" life. I spent a lot of time on that front. As a result of my newfound project, I was basically always recovering from drinking beer the night before.

I would jump from one cheap happy hour to the next with my college acquaintances, waiting for something to happen, which remains my least favorite sensation. My friend Jason, then a talent manager, invited me to media parties. On the way to one of those parties, where Jason said he wanted to introduce me to someone named Lena Dunham (this was before *Girls*), I found two pairs of Gap pants in my size on the subway. I was headed to one of *n+1*'s (the literary magazine) then-legendary parties. I left the pants in their plastic drawstring Gap bag, then, too tipsy to remember my pre-party fluke, left the bag at the party. The next day, I emailed the magazine about my lost pants. Apparently the note was a hit, because it's the only time other than this book and my high school yearbook that Laura Mayer's words have appeared in print, in the Letters to the Editor section of the magazine.

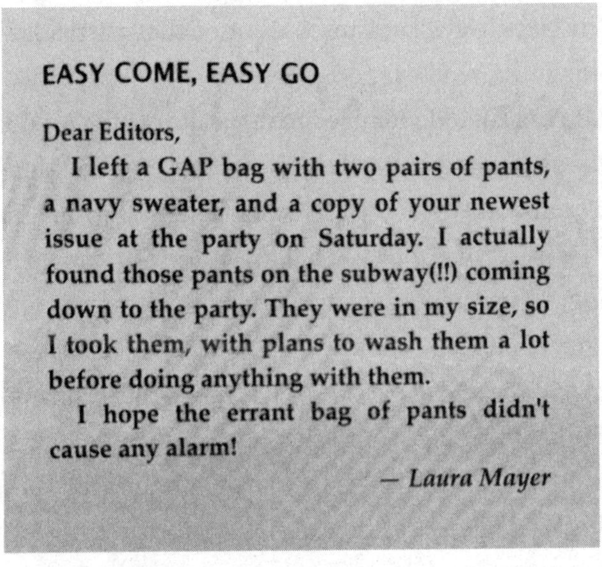

EASY COME, EASY GO

Dear Editors,

I left a GAP bag with two pairs of pants, a navy sweater, and a copy of your newest issue at the party on Saturday. I actually found those pants on the subway(!!) coming down to the party. They were in my size, so I took them, with plans to wash them a lot before doing anything with them.

I hope the errant bag of pants didn't cause any alarm!

— Laura Mayer

I never got those pants back.

One time I accidentally went to a rave and ended up in a stairwell, head in my hands, already hungover at 3:00 a.m., wondering why my friends were taking so long to stop dancing. This was before Lyft, before Uber. You hailed a town car deep in Brooklyn and hoped they were an unlicensed taxi—and not a random driver looking to take a drunk girl on a ride—so that they'd take twenty dollars to spill you back in front of your apartment, or you called Eastern Car Service and hoped they'd show up to that part of Bushwick at that time of morning.

"Your friends are on drugs," a professional chandelier designer told me, slinking beside me on the stairwell.

"Oh," I said.

Now it all started making sense. Of course they were on drugs! I always kept myself out of that particular loop, thankfully.

Then Mr. Chandelier tried to make out with me. I obliged.

When you are young, drunk, and in a stairwell in Bushwick, someone will try to make out with you. This is practically a rule of physics. Particularly if they're a professional chandelier designer. During that time, I ran into, and made out with, a lot of Mr. Chandeliers.

Toward the end of my haze days, I got a tattoo on my back, which has since faded into two blocks of murky black text, that says "Something will happen sometime soon." An ode to putting it all out there and waiting for a return.

That tattoo, which now looks more like a QR code, represented all the tryhard energy boiling inside of me that had no specific place to go. At that time I felt like I was taking poorly thought-out, half-hearted shots into the ether, hoping for results. I was impersonating being young and carefree, never embodying it.

And it's not like ambition protects tryhards. Ambition is not a centrifugal force. Tryhards can go sideways like everyone else. Think of Elizabeth Holmes, Dick Cheney, or that astronaut who drove nonstop cross-country while wearing government-issued astronaut diapers to confront her ex-lover's girlfriend. As an aside, you must be a tryhard to become an astronaut.

If I were more honest, I'd put this time on my résumé and highlight it in yellow. It was as valuable as all the future promotions and job titles combined.

More truth: I was just as bad at work as I was at socializing, that first year at WNYC. The job with Sara Fishko was terribly easy and still I managed to blow it most days when I first started. The job involved transcribing interviews, writing interview prep documents, going into the homes of elderly musicians and writers who were the topics of the series to record interviews Sara conducted over the phone. That's called a tape sync: The gopher (me) went in-person to record the interview sound in high-quality, while my boss spoke to the guests from the comfort of her office. It's not uncommon for expert interviewers, which Sara is, to conduct interviews from afar. Terry Gross, for example, is rarely in-studio with the people she interviews.

No part of the job came easily to me. I couldn't write an email to save my life. I'd routinely do errands for Sara—picking up limited-edition CDs of very specific types of music, generally from the 1940s or '50s, from archivists for her pieces, as an example—and frantically return, only to realize that I forgot to check if the CD was actually in the envelope. I returned to Sara with an empty envelope at least three times. I cried in her office because I knew I was so bad at my job. Sara was exacting, but she gave me the grace to be twenty-two, to fail and try again. Because, as she told me recently, she knew I wanted the job. She knew I was determined.

She knew things I'd temporarily forgotten: that I could be competent.

卌 II

Job 7

Side-Hustling

> **Keep carrots away from soil that has recently had manure added into it, or they may grow "legs" . . .**
>
> *The Old Farmer's Almanac 2015*

My husband, Danny, has one beauty product he swears by. It's called O'Keeffe's Working Hands, a solution meant for the *toughest* of hands. A balm that guarantees relief. Relief from the calluses formed from lifting wood, drilling things, forcefully lugging items, etc. Things Danny doesn't do outside of moving from one apartment to another every few years. And yet, he applies and reapplies O'Keeffe's Working Hands daily. It comes in a green plastic puck with a prominent capital-*G* guarantee of relief. Twist it open to reveal a thick, Crisco-like white ointment. A viscous balm. Maybe even a salve? When applied, it coats your hands in a layer of greasy pomade that seems to just sit on the skin's surface, buffering it from the elements, rather than sinking into one's hand meat. If you've got Working Hands on your working hands, then prepare for it to get on everything you own.

The problem with O'Keeffe's Working Hands—and anything, I contend, meant to moisturize—is that the only way to maintain that level of moisture is by constantly reapplying. Working Hands has you back twisting the puck, reapplying its unctuous cream, returning to your computer, smearing it all over your keyboard and body, every hour on the hour.

I applied some of this before I sat down to write these paragraphs. As I type this, I can feel my hands drying, the pull for more Working Hands strong. I'm not heeding its call. And, as you can tell, I think body lotions are a crock of shit. Particularly for hands, the part of the body where age and effort can never be hidden. Me? My hands have looked like the crypt keeper's ever since I was old enough to have knuckles.

I speak of hands because they're a universal tool for human work. From stacking blocks to reading a book to lifting lumber to, say, typing a memoir, our claws are what empower us to *do*. And they reveal the wear and tear of labor before any other body part.

When Grand-ma-ma (never "Grandma"), my mom's

mom, died in 2000, she had one hell of an open-casket Irish Catholic wake and funeral. There were tons of bagpipes. There were also tons of people. Tons of flowers. Tons of handcrafted handkerchiefs tucked within each of the funeral programs.

Cut to the open casket.

"They did a good job on her makeup," my aunt said.

"Her hair looks good," another aunt said.

"A shame they couldn't young-up her hands," my mom said.

I now understand, twenty-plus years later, that the window to the soul is not, in fact, the eyes. Cosmetic surgery technology hasn't cracked the case on how to "young-up" hands. Even AI is famously bad at creating accurate images of hands or fingers.

By the time Grand-ma-ma died I'd been to a lot of open-casket Irish wakes. My paternal grandmother, Nana Mayer, had a lot of friends and, as she got older, her friends up and died on her. So to the wakes we went. If there's one thing the Irish love it's getting drunk and gossiping in full view of an embalmed, shiny corpse in their Sunday Mass best.

Second cousins got loose. Everyone was named Kelly, Mary-Anne, or Ginger, and they were all drinking whiskey in the middle of the afternoon. Positively toasted, celebrating the life of the waxy body in the corner of the room. "This is a good way to go out," they said about the elders who died, the same as they did at every wake. I didn't really know any of the dead guests of honor until my mom's mom, Grand-ma-ma, a.k.a. Margaret Reilly, died. From my memory, Grand-ma-ma died suddenly. I was very sad.

My mother gave me sixty dollars after I cried in her car when she told me her mom died. Not sure what to do with my feelings, I was given a grief allowance. A few days later we drove out to Iowa for the wake and funeral. I hadn't seen my mom's sisters or my cousins since I was very young. Everyone was sad: Grand-ma-ma died at sixty-eight. "Too young," and "Not a good way to go out," everyone said. At thirty-eight, I agree. At twelve, I remember thinking, *I don't know—that's pretty old.*

My Grand-ma-ma's hands were also working ones. She worked every day of her life: as the mother of five, at a succession of jobs, as a caretaker for my sometimes troubled grandfather. One of the only early baby photos I've seen of my mother is her visiting Grand-ma-ma in the break room of her job at "the radiation research lab" in Alaska, or so it's written on the bottom of the photo. And, as I discovered while eating cabbage and wandering around the wake, she wasn't done working when she died. Standing proudly, as the centerpiece on a table full of family photos, was Grand-ma-ma's datebook. Full of birthdays, to-do lists, and work commitments, all filled out months into the future. Margaret Reilly was not a woman who was planning to die, and this planner proved it. Paging through the book made it clear that she had shit to do. Child logic held on to this detail, hard. I assumed I'd missed all the other datebooks at the many other wakes I'd ever attended.

While working at *Slate* magazine when I was twenty-eight, I casually mentioned "the traditional wake datebook" to an editor, a fellow Irish Catholic.

His eyes widened as he said, "What . . . are you talking about?"

"You can't young-up hands" stuck with me, too. The condition of one's hands is second only to the condition of one's teeth in projecting status—age, professional standing, income, you name it. Though porcelain-veneer technology has advanced at warp speed for teeth, you always know the jig is up for a Real Housewife when they start wearing gloves during the summer in the Hamptons. Professional appearances became incredibly important to me as I entered the working world. While I felt like a feral chaos Muppet with working hands, I determined I must look as if I were a motivated young professional who worked effortlessly, with immaculate nail beds, on the outside. Cut my cuticles, please!

I started getting manicures at twenty-two years old because my investment banker roommate did so every Sunday afternoon, and she had her shit together when her hangovers wore off. I kept getting manicures because I enjoyed the feeling of a stranger holding my hand. It's an almost romantic exchange when you're as lonely as I was when I first moved to New York. I particularly enjoyed seeing this one manicurist who, without fail, would look at my short nails and exclaim "What nails?!" I went to her exclusively for a year. Maternal cutting.

I stayed away from pedicures for a while. A friendly stranger seeing my foot—a foot that's basically hard skeleton with a skin sock on—was too intimate. I call my feet my lizards because they snarl, a.k.a. hurt, constantly. I've got working hands and flat feet. I'd tend to my toenails once a month with the joy that one would take in changing the dressing on a wound. Then one Sunday while getting a manicure, I noticed *the working women on laptops getting pedicures.* I immediately idolized them and invented the stories of their lives. Their ponytails swished in the air as their yet-to-be polished nails flew across their keyboards. I imagined TWWOLGP hauled their Lenovos with them to the nail salon after waking up early, exercising, finishing their chores, and socializing an appropriate amount. It was time for them to bring their hands and feet to their level: They were prepared for the office battlefield, all they needed was a little varnishing. They'd post up in those massage chairs over the whirlpool foot baths and crank out spreadsheets. Before the workweek even had begun there they were, already, ahead of it. After I discovered TWWOLGP, I started getting pedicures, too. Because I wanted to be one of them.

Though, I will say, the first time I brought my laptop to the nail salon I dropped it in the foot bath. I screamed. This was before reliable wi-fi; I'm not sure what work I was even planning on doing with my laptop. Open up a Microsoft Word document and place a blinking cursor on it, waiting for something to happen?

Except, sitting silently staring into space has never been my strong suit, so I would stare at that cursor.

During this era of my work life I had a full-time job at New York Public Radio. I wasn't making enough money. I could barely pay my rent, eat some, pay for a manicure, and buy one pack of cigarettes a week. I started looking into what would later be branded as side hustles to close the gap. But all my ideas were particularly personally punishing.

For one, I became convinced I could be a day-of wedding coordinator. Despite having no interest in weddings, there's nothing I love more than coordinating. But what this job actually entails is less coordinating and more bearing with an endless hell that is wrought upon you, for a short period of time. Day-of wedding coordinators tend to work with high-end wedding planners, who work for high-net-worth individuals, who are looking to combine assets via a legally binding party known as a wedding. Wedding planners can work with their clients for years. Day-of wedding coordinators come in when all the details are set, right before the curtain comes up. So, that's to say, when all of the details start to fall apart. In 2010 you could make upward of $5,000 for two days of getting screamed at by a wedding planner, a bride, a groom, and an entire bridal party. Many pennies for your ears. This sounded perfect. Despite trying, though, I couldn't get an in with a wedding planner.

Another idea: fit modeling. I weighed precisely zero pounds during this period of my life, thanks to the cigarettes and low food budget. I looked into fit modeling, specifically for petite pants. Fit models are sentient mannequins, meant to stand still while clothing makers test out their clothes on a realistic human body, prior to selling them to actual human bodies in stores and online. Turns out my stature (five foot two) makes me short, even for a petite fit model. Plus, my inseam is that of a piglet. I'm all torso—my guts have plenty of room. But I don't fit the common petite consumer. So the plan to be a headless wax statue was out.

Fit modeling brought me into the wide world of parts modeling. Parts modeling is exactly what it sounds like: models who specialize in certain parts of the body, rather than the whole shebang: legs, feet, eyes, hands, etc. The most holistic you get as a parts model is if you're offering up your full torso ("even skin tone, well-toned and nice muscularity" are the requirements, according to Parts Models, the leading parts model management company). To the extent that I have any physical appeal, it's in the gestalt. You gotta see the whole thing together. But during the course of my parts modeling research, I became completely obsessed with hand models. As an intellectual rather than operational exercise (see: my crypt keeper hands since I was a child).

Hand models are paid for their time on the shoot, sure.

But they are the Olympians of parts models. They must make their hands their full-time jobs. Sure, there are manicures. But I'm talking about the daily training: the moisturizing (Working Hands is not a product I came across in my research, for what it's worth, *Danny*), the protection (wearing gloves at all times), washing hands only when needed. For a hand model, a paper cut could mean a significant loss of income. Being a successful hand model requires vigilance and planning at all times. Vigilance and planning, my love languages.

Then, there were the sham immigration marriages. As a US citizen in the early 2010s, there was no shortage of wealthy young men looking to secure a green card or citizenship through marrying someone like me. That is, someone looking for some cash and unlikely to get married any time soon. There were two sham marriage proposals I considered: one to an Australian I called Dracula, with whom I occasionally made out. The other was to a college friend who wanted to stay in the States. They both offered me the same deal: $10,000, no strings attached. I made the mistake of telling my father about these "business opportunities," and he made me aware of the tax implications and also suggested "Don't you think you could do better than ten thousand dollars?" And "What if you actually get married?" I wasn't so concerned about the latter. I turned both offers down for bureaucratic reasons. I attended the eventual sham (or perhaps non-sham?) wedding of Dracula. While sitting on the floor of a warehouse in Brooklyn during the reception, the bride came up to me and told me to "get my hands off her husband." My hands were not near her husband, I said, literally putting my working hands in front of my face.

And finally, there was the unpaid work that I thought would lead to paid work—making radio stories for a show called *Too Much Information* on the local community-run radio station WFMU. I shudder to think of the audio essays I turned in to the host, Benjamen Walker. He was tough on me, told me when ideas were bad, and showed me how to do things better. For a year I worked nights and weekends, for free, to help produce his show.

During that time, I lived in an apartment above an Italian restaurant in Hell's Kitchen, with an investment banker and the assistant to a famed literary agent. My roommates were never around. Who were around? Dozens of mice. The super gave me glue traps and told me to put peanut butter on top of them to lure the mice. Problem was, the glue traps didn't kill the mice. They just broke their legs. I'd come home from my day job and murder twelve, thirteen mice a day. I did this by putting another glue trap on top of the mouse and slamming a coffee-table book on top of them (per the super's orders). I then put the mice in garbage bags and ran downstairs to throw them out in the trash can outside a Starbucks.

At night, I worked on the podcast. I remember hearing the mice scurry around and feeling less alone—even though I knew I'd eventually have to murder them. One of those audio essays was about killing more than one hundred mice in that apartment, and the essay got into the ears of one Daniel Blondell. Danny made his way into my email inbox. I ignored him. We later ran into each other at a bar while I was dancing with an elderly man.

He went up to me and asked, “Are you Laura Mayer?”

I asked him if he was trying to serve me with a lawsuit. And the rest is history.

Yes, I worked for love. How else would I have found it, really?

Job 8

Faster and Faster, More and More

> **Beer makes you feel the way you ought to feel without beer.**
>
> Henry Lawson, Australian writer

The only thing that slowed down this tryhard between the ages of eighteen and twenty-five was alcohol, which had finally come to see what I would give it.

The first time I drank alcohol was in my friend Karen's dorm room, before a football game in fall quarter of freshman year. I remember thinking, *So this is the big deal?*

I'd avoided drinking in high school for two reasons: (1) The effect I saw it had on my parents, my mom in particular, and (2) I never had the opportunity, socially. When you apply to enroll in the neighborhood narc court, Peer Jury, turns out the party invites don't flow in.

After that first drink in the dorms, I dabbled—at frat parties, with various boyfriends, later at a club or two (I once owned multiple tube tops).

For the first two years, I didn't get it. And then, junior year of college, I had a boyfriend and my drinking began as a game of playing catch-up with his. Quickly, it morphed entirely into my own game.

I was meeting all these new people through that boyfriend, which made me socially anxious. Alcohol, of course, works remarkably well for social anxiety. And so, the cycle repeated.

I knew and I didn't know what I was entering.

In college I wrote my journalism thesis on a comedian and a recovering addict who chaired her home group's Narcotics Anonymous meetings. I was curious about the nature of anonymity in recovery groups—why the secrecy when fellowships saved so many lives? It was, again, an attempt to understand the silence and denial around addiction in my family. I spent three months following her around—watching comedy sets, seeing her perform theater, and attending NA meetings. Media is forbidden at such meetings. I was a journalism student, and this piece (thank God) would never be published. But I think the comedian could tell I was struggling with something related to substance abuse.

I never revealed this to her, but I've found that if you've gone through recovery, you can intuit when someone like me (twenty-one, an endless pit of questions related to a very specific topic, who sat in awe with them in their apartment for months) is trying to work something out in a similar space.

Her time and generosity in introducing me to the fellowship made my eventual dips into various fellowships years later much easier. It's those bits of generosity that stick with me, that I think about on most nights while I'm brushing my teeth or falling asleep (ideally, those aren't the same activities). She doesn't know I feel this way, but maybe I should schedule an email about it.

When I moved to New York a year later I still had the urge to figure out addiction, to understand it from my mother's point of view and, increasingly, from my own. So, I got to work. Name a recovery memoir published between the years 1985 and 2025, and I've read it.

The soothing part and the frustrating part of the "addiction memoir" category is that many of the narratives exist in precisely the same shape: open with the rock-bottom moment; back up to a childhood that laid the groundwork for the future addiction; several active addiction stories; route back to the rock bottom; introduce entrance(s) into recovery; and then a slow reintroduction into society as a changed person.

Drinking: A Love Story by Caroline Knapp remains my

favorite recovery memoir, by far. Knapp wrote it at thirty-six years old, in the mid-nineties, the precise age when my hard hustling in media was in full swing. When I read it, at twenty-three, it felt like reading a deeply revealing diary from an older sister I never had, about insecurities I couldn't yet name in myself and perceptions I was fighting to prop up. Knapp and I also shared some things in common: We both came from fine towns, went to nice colleges, pursued careers in journalism, and had an alcoholic parent.

"In some families alcohol washes across whole generations, a liquid plague," she wrote, and I nodded.

"Alcohol is everywhere in your life, omnipresent, and you're both aware and unaware of it almost all the time; all you know is you'd die without it, and there is no simple reason why this happens, no single moment, no physiological event that pushes a heavy drinker across a concrete line into alcoholism. It's a slow, gradual, insidious, elusive *becoming*," she wrote.

From the moment I moved to New York to the time I stopped drinking, I sowed small bits of chaos wherever I went—which was to happy hours, parties, and after parties. I was occasionally, depending on the evening, the life of the party. I dated my way through Bushwick's least eligible bachelors. I was often part of a group of the last people to leave a party. My friend Jason and I would stage fake fights when we were bored—yelling loudly at each other in someone's kitchen. Memorably, we posted up near a kitchen island after arriving at some friend-of-a-friend's co-op and began yelling back and forth: "It's MY MAGAZINE! How dare you try to take MY MAGAZINE job at a time like THIS!"

One time, while he was wearing a fur coat he found in a dumpster, Jason got bored at a New Year's party and deliberately threw himself down a flight of stairs as a joke. I laughed until I puked. Jason was fine—he fell gracefully. No one else thought it was funny.

I never was not at least a little bit hungover. But I was so young that no one could tell.

* * *

I stopped drinking after an unremarkable party at which I drank too much and spoke too extensively to some archivist at MTV. She told me, by way of getting out of the conversation, "Yeah, you should write a PhD on [whatever topic I was talking about]." What an amazing insult!

When I got back to my apartment that night, the first apartment I shared with Danny, I had one last glass of wine, alone in the kitchen. I didn't even bother turning on the light. I woke up the next morning hungover and late to meet a friend. I looked at my cat Hector, while cringing both at the PhD comment (which, to this day, I still look for opportunities to steal), but mostly at the drinking alone in the dark after the party. What was I trying to satisfy? What would those kinds of moments turn into? Then, I thought, *Maybe I should stop drinking.* So I stopped, eleven days before my twenty-sixth birthday.

"The problem with self-transformation is that after a while, you don't know which version of yourself to believe in, which one is true," Knapp wrote in *Drinking*.

When my mom was drinking, it made me consider the "version" of her I thought I'd never know. But perhaps I had not missed out on the real version of her after all. Perhaps, they were all her.

And perhaps the same is true of me, the tryhard who is rarely home, always working. This is the addiction I found while dodging another, the one I developed by becoming myself—or the version of myself I am right now.

I reread *Drinking: A Love Story* this week, from the vantage point of someone who is sober from alcohol but still feels the gnaw of want, of filling the existential hole, which I now recognize I satisfy through my office job and here, on this very page you're reading.

卌 ||||

Job 9

Mentoring

Any account of the loyalty of young hearts to some exalted ideal, and the passion with which they strive, will always, in some of us, rekindle generous emotions.

Willa Cather, *The Song of the Lark*

There are certain jobs that refuse to go anywhere. Often this is true of a first job.

Fishko Files at WNYC was an interminable loop. I spoke to my boss, Sara, on the phone and through the glass of her office, ten feet away. Sometimes she'd ask me for my opinion on the HBO show *Girls*, whose auteur, Lena Dunham, I could've met a year earlier if I weren't so concerned about finding my free pants. I transcribed interviews and transcribed some more. Sara produced her shows, and I watched. It was all very civilized. She didn't need me, and I needed to be needed. I was sober, alert, stuck, and my compass was pointing "out."

The only bright spot was my desk location. I sat in the same office bay as *On the Media*, a nationally distributed NPR program with a focus on how journalism does and doesn't work. One day, four years into my time at WNYC, the executive producer, sensing my imminent departure, asked to borrow me. She said I could pitch a story for her show.

These were magic words.

I had a story I wanted to tell! Lots of them! Something was happening!

The story I pitched to the executive producer of *On the Media* that week was central to a passion of mine: reality television. Namely, the entrancing yet often painfully mundane franchises like *The Real Housewives*, *Vanderpump Rules*, and *The Bachelor*. Shows that throw hot people into heavily lit Jacuzzis and wait for the magic to happen.

The fabulous detail I wanted *On the Media* listeners to be aware of was this: No matter how voluminous the heads of hair, how flashy the cars, how blue the twinkling eye, or even (and maybe especially) how incredibly beautiful the characters, reality TV would be deadly boring without wildly manipulative music cues.

Imagine this scene. A camera lays its gaze on one woman's resting face; the camera then whips to another woman's resting face as a soundalike of *The Phantom of the Opera* overture blares. This manufactured moment can propel an entire episode—sometimes an entire season, pitting two women with neutral expressions against each other.

My ten-minute story went deep on how the music for reality television was made, how it moved plot, why it mattered.

This was not hard-hitting journalism, nothing like what I imagined I might make once unleashed as a creative in the radio world. But one starts by making what one knows.

The week after the segment aired, Danny (then-boyfriend, soon-to-be husband) and I were at the Bronx Zoo. Just two mid-twenties DINKs taking advantage of Wednesday's free admission. It was one hundred degrees, humid, and we were wandering the Madagascar exhibit when I received an email from my first ever fan (Danny excluded, because he was trying to marry me):

> Dear Ms. Mayer,
>
> My name is Libby Lastname. I'm a high school student from Long Island. I listened to your recent report on WNYC, New York Public Radio. I am interested in radio production and would love the opportunity to shadow you at the radio station.
>
> Sincerely, Libby Lastname, an actual child

This was truly astonishing. Someone had heard my story and been moved to reach out. I had influenced the heart and mind of at least one public-radio-loving youth! I conferred with Danny and waited fifteen minutes before replying—to keep my desperation for approval in check.

"Libby Lastname," I wrote, "of course you're welcome to shadow me. I'm happy that you enjoyed 'You're Being Manipulated by Reality TV (Music).' It was a real thinker!"

The next day, I darted back to work with the good news, and Libby's request to shadow me was approved. It took several more months to arrange the particulars, but my first fan finally arrived on a blustery day that winter.

The temperature is significant, because Libby Lastname was wearing very little clothing: a short, pleated lacrosse skirt, a white polo, and one high heel. One high heel because her other foot was in a medical boot. The outfit was topped with a single crutch. At six feet tall, the ensemble was striking. Libby Lastname also brought along a classmate I'll call Vivi. Nowhere in my email correspondence with Libby was Vivi mentioned. Vivi was dressed similarly, though with heels, and no crutch.

It must've seemed as if I were inviting two heavily disinterested coeds to rush the public-radio sorority, as I walked them around. Their boredom, from the moment Libby and Vivi threw down their overnight bags, was extreme. It was as if they'd been sentenced to a stretch in jail with me as their warden.

I tentatively held on to my excitement (I still have a fan—maybe two!) and placed Libby at a desk, and Vivi at the one next to it. I made sure Libby's crutch was within reach. Then I talked them through the one-day public-radio curriculum I'd developed over the months we spent organizing the visit:

1. Introduction to audio editing! I selected raw audio from the previous week's show and instructed them to play around with the audio editing software to clean up the interview.

2. Introduction to host prep documents! One of *On the Media*'s cohosts had an interview later that day. I was producing the interview and wrote the prep document ahead of time. But, for Libby and Vivi's sake, I prepared a collection of news articles on the segment's subject and encouraged them to think of any questions they'd want our host to ask the guest. "Follow your curiosity!"

3. Introduction to a live, in-studio interview! After they completed their prep document, we were going to sit together in the control room and listen to the interview the host conducted with the guest.

A crash course in radio making, my young fans!

I'm not convinced wildly manipulative music cues could have enlivened the scene that afternoon: two hyper-disinterested teens furiously chomping and snapping bubble gum, interrupted at random moments by their chirpy mentor and guide.

They seemed relieved every time I shut my mouth.

Somewhere along the way, I'd miscalculated. Or did I do too much, yet again? How had I managed to overwhelm a fellow public-radio obsessive?

The day continued. Libby and Vivi looked up from their phones and agreed to come sit in the control room to listen to our host conduct the interview. As soon as we stopped rolling on the interview, Libby and Vivi stood up and exited the control room without a word and went right back to their desks and their phones.

There are many things I miss from working in public radio in 2014. The main one being that people spoke to each other—often at high volumes—with their actual voices. The eavesdropping! Now everyone Slacks and gossips in digital silos. That afternoon there was a lull in production, and our intern asked me if I was going to a monthly public-radio meetup that night. I said I had other plans (holding my cat Hector, petting him, feeding him, "talking" in "his voice" to Danny), but Libby and Vivi shot their gazes up from their phones.

"Party?!" they said, practically in unison.

Our intern offered to take them to the bar where the event would be held. Libby and Vivi, suddenly perky, started texting even more urgently.

The next morning, our intern asked to speak to me privately.

"So, last night, with Libby and Vivi . . ." she began.

"Are they alive?!" I asked, immediately fired up by maternal worry.

"Yes, they're alive. Libby Lastname sent me a text before she got on the train to Long Island."

"Well, what did the text say?"

"Uh . . . It said 'Cocaine is a helluva drug.'"

Turns out the purehearted public-radio obsessive, Libby Lastname, whom I created in my mind, and my mind only, had used me shamelessly to acquire her target: older men, drugs, and a good time in the city while Mom and Dad thought she was safe with public-radio nerds. The intern let them have one beer a piece, and the next time she saw them they had smoky makeup around their eyes and were headed out to meet some guys in Murray Hill (or, as I once called that neighborhood, Blurry Hill, because that was one of the places to party with investment bankers on weeknights). The intern learned that Libby and Vivi had been texting these men the entire day. They'd met them on a seeking-arrangements website. The arrangement with the men: Libby and Vivi show up as the high school students they are; the men get them helluva drugs.

Libby and Vivi's arrangement with me: the perfect cover story for going into New York City.

I still think about Libby Lastname and Vivi. I know they got home safely, because they kept texting our intern, answering various "Are you okay?" and "Are you still okay?"

messages I funneled through the intern. I think about how perfectly hatched their plan was. How many people did they email to get to me, so eager for approval? Was I that easy of a mark? Such a clear conduit for Libby Lastname to get what she wanted? I can only assume that Libby Lastname is now the wily CEO of a skyrocketing fintech start-up. She deserves it. I would put that maneuver on my résumé.

卌 卌

Job 10

Leaving on Time

> **If you still have a problem, check that all cables are connected and then try again.**
>
> IKEA instructions

My brush with two Long Island teenage "fans" and one well-received radio story didn't change the dead-end nature of my job. Since I was personally settled—sober, cohabiting, a fifty-fifty owner of an IKEA couch—I had to turn my energy elsewhere.

Often, when I feel stuck, I look for things that delight me (and are, generally, completely unrelated to the job at hand). I then put my full weight behind getting involved with the delight target. It makes me laugh and feel like I am doing something with my time. And, sometimes, the forward momentum of a purehearted scheme unleashes a type of movement I didn't know I could achieve.

I call this move "procrastin-action."

For procrastin-action to work, the action has to be tied to positive feelings that you uniquely respond to. For me, I like giggling wildly to myself, often alone at a computer. I like low-stakes spectacles. I like involving others in the pursuit, inviting them to the sideshow. I don't like embarrassing myself, exactly, but I know that embarrassment motivates me. Embarrassment is nothing if not the visceral reaction to making yourself vulnerable, to putting yourself out there, which I wasn't doing in pretty much any area of my life at that time.

The year 2013 was a simpler time. For one, it was more than a decade ago. Things have happened to you and to me and to this country since then, therefore it seems simpler by comparison. But, most important, brands hadn't yet figured out how to interact with social media.

Now brands have fully developed "voices," with content plans, project-management systems, and often multiple team members. Right at this very moment, Taco Bell, Wendy's, Oreos, you name it, are trying to be funny on the internet. But, before the social media brand industrial complex, there was Red Lobster's LobStar of the Week Facebook contest.

In the early 2010s Red Lobster saw an opportunity. In the

earliest days of Facebook someone created a community for people who loved Cheddar Bay Biscuits. If you've ever been to a Red Lobster, you know what I'm talking about: the unlimited cheese-infused biscuits you get with every meal. That, plus water, plus a cup of chowder, makes for a full feast on a budget. Red Lobster identified the organic internet biscuit interest and took advantage. And that's when the fun started.

Every week, Red Lobster's rabid fan base would post photos of themselves at Red Lobster. Then, through some combination of "thumbs-ups" and, I deduced, the Wizard of Oz running Big Lobster's page-making decisions, a LobStar of the Week was chosen and celebrated. Babies won most of the time. Knowing what I know now about babies and shellfish exposure, I'm even more suspect of these entrants. Elderly couples in love eating crabs were another winning combination. Pets occasionally snuck in there, in photos taken *off-site*, which I found to be a form of chicanery. Occasionally, winners would use Red Lobster's food in their entries: a crab-claw high five, a lobster tail tossed in the air, a shrimp smile.

The formula was clear: Shellfish plus action equaled a LobStar of the Week.

You might be wondering, *What did the LobStar of the week win, exactly?* Well, nothing, precisely. Except for adulation among other Red Lobster fans on the Red Lobster Facebook page. I was in it for the adulation. And I became single-mindedly determined to win.

Not a baby, nor an elderly couple in love, and unwilling to bring my cat to Red Lobster, I knew my food prop work was going to be important. I also needed a photographer. Before the era of the Instagram/TikTok boyfriend, I enlisted Danny to come with me to Red Lobster in Times Square, a flagship location, on Valentine's Day. Valentine's Day: the ultimate news peg for lobster lovers.

The Red Lobster in Times Square in 2013 had another name: hell. There was a lower-level bar full of tourists and older businessmen who seemed to be looking to score more than some popcorn shrimp. Nothing got the juices flowing more than getting tanked next to a murky, well, tank of miscellaneous sea creatures that you hoped, for everyone's sake, wouldn't end up in your soup.

For some, the bar was the destination. For most, the lower level was the holding pen in which you clutched one of those vibrating plastic pucks, eager for the main event.

Our puck beckoned us, and we were brought upstairs. I had a $75 gift card. The floor was packed with families, and lots of people on Valentine's dates. I knew that to win LobStar of the Week, a storyline would be helpful. So I exploited the opportunity of this being Danny and my first Valentine's Day together, and worked that into the narrative. We ordered as many varieties of seafood as possible for the photos: lobster, shrimp, flounder, scallops.

That Monday, I submitted my LobStar of the Week photos (I went with a "shrimp smile") and the details of a new couple choosing to spend their Valentine's Day at Red Lobster.

I then emailed virtually everyone I knew, asking them to like my post, spent a then-ungodly sum of fourteen dollars for two rounds of Facebook promotion, and waited.

That Thursday night I got a text from a coworker that simply said, "You did it." More messages flooded in from friends and acquaintances who I'd conscripted into my win: "You're an inspiration!" "I was weirdly invested in you winning LobStar" "She won the internet."

Ten years later I was on a Zoom call with someone who I had known at WNYC. Both of us had moved on to different jobs by then. She said to me, "You always seemed so quiet. But I knew after the LobStar thing that I needed to know you."

* * *

On a different day, well after Libby and Vivi had left, after I was coronated LobStar of the Week, the host of *On the Media* took me aside and said, "It's time for a new job." Not in a *You're bad at your job* sense. But in a *There's no more opportunity for you* way. Or that's how I interpreted it.

"That made me laugh, actually, because everyone could see you needed a new job," Katya, the executive producer, told me recently. So when an opportunity came for me to be the first employee of a podcast start-up, I hung up my microphone and went into management for good . . . or so I thought.

卌 卌 |

Job 11

Coveting Thy Neighbor

I see this, and hate this, and dread this, and don't know but that money might make a much worse change in me. And yet I have money always in my thoughts and my desires; and the whole life I place before myself is money, money, money, and what money can make of life!

Charles Dickens, *Our Mutual Friend*

There is a moment in the life of any tryhard when you move from wanting a seat at the table to wanting to own the actual table.

I live in Ditmas Park, Brooklyn. If you google the neighborhood, you'll see photos upon photos of gorgeous Victorian homes. Tree-lined streets. Maybe you'll click into a People.com article and see that Michelle Williams (the actress) once lived here. The author Jonathan Safran Foer is rumored to live in a manse on the most mansion-y street. There's a chalkboard outside of the house with poetry written on it. I've stuck my nose past the poetry board to admire the lavish water feature in the maybe-Foer side yard.

Side yards. Imagine having so much space, so much lawn, that it doesn't fit into a front and a back yard? No, it spills over to the side. Unnecessary, decadent, unsightly if not maintained: the side boob of landscaping.

The only other time I've used the words *side yard* in a sentence was when texting with my father, Bob Mayer. I asked what he did that day. He told me he was hiking along the train tracks in Glencoe to collect tadpoles in a bucket to put in "the side yard."

"The side yard?" I said, knowing that the house I grew up in, in suburban Chicago, had a sliver of front and some back, but absolutely no side yard.

"Where the pond is," he said.

Now I realized he meant the low-lying land that often flooded. The grass that crept between his property line and his longtime neighbor's—and often nemesis's—house.

"You're trying to grow frogs in Becky's yard?"

"A plague of frogs," he said.

Knowing what little you know of Bob Mayer now, it makes

sense that his daughter moved to the Big City only to hard-lookie-loo the side yards of literary celebrities.

But Safran Foer's house wasn't my top obsession. I've long had my eye on a different house: a beautiful, gray, compact Tudor two blocks away from my rental apartment. This house isn't on manse row. It's tucked away on a side street, among other very nice houses. It's modest compared to its larger neighbors, compact, recently painted, carefully trimmed, a thick-paned bay window, with a widow's walk and stained-glass flourishes. Built in the 1800s, it's what a real estate agent would call "lovingly remodeled" and actually mean it. According to publicly available property records with photos, the current owners didn't gut the house. But they did give it a good polishing and one of those hard dental hygienist flossings that uncovers the brilliance lurking beneath years of stains. But, the original teeth still remain.

The Gray House, as I call it, isn't just a gray house—it's a gray *home*. There are signs of life, of movement. On the front door the owners taped four cut-out faces—a family art project where, I imagine, the parents didn't interfere too much with what their kids drew. I've never gotten close enough, or worn my glasses enough, to see, but I imagine they're a depiction of each of the family members. Mom, Dad, two kids. They have a sensible minivan that comes and goes, parked in their driveway ready to go—rather than stowed in their detached garage, used only for visits to their country house.

During the earliest days of the pandemic, when we were still disinfecting groceries but not yet wearing masks, I'd get up at 6:00 a.m. and take cold spring walks up and down the streets. Down dead ends. Down manse row. And, of course, past the Gray House. I wondered what they were doing there. How they were faring. If they were considering putting up a pleading sign, like a different neighbor did, in a front window saying something like "WE ARE SO BORED." How does a family, seemingly so vibrant in and outside of their home with their minivan, grind to a halt?

I still walk by the Gray House (on the other side of the street; I'm not a freak) at least once a week. My singular obsession with this house, and with homeownership and what it represents (stability), consumes much of my time. It's what I work for.

卌 卌 ||

Job 12

Getting Sucked In

Soon, too soon, I entered the giddy whirl.

Mary Wollstonecraft Shelley, *The Last Man*

In October 2014, which marked my fifth autumn in New York, a little podcast called *Serial* premiered.

I was right in the middle of the monastic weekend experiences of my mid-twenties, which mostly involved organizing my sweaters followed by washing four laundry loads at LaundryCity laundromat, when I fired up the first episode.

In case you were busy plugging your ears in 2014, *Serial* is about the murder of a teenage girl named Hae Min Lee, focused almost entirely on the guilt or innocence of the accused, her boyfriend, Adnan Syed.

I was hooked before the theme music ended (music by Nick Thorburn, from Islands and the Unicorns, a college-era musical obsession). That was the case for about ten million other listeners, too.

It would be accurate to call me a longtime true-crime junkie. I convinced my sixth-grade teacher to allow me to write a book report on Truman Capote's grisly *In Cold Blood*. I began watching *20/20* and *Dateline*—on my own—as soon as I could operate the remote.

While high-brow, high-production-value, true-crime podcasts and TV shows are ubiquitous now, they were not a hugely familiar offering in 2014. Netflix, Hulu, and HBO had not begun cranking out documentaries about murdered women and/or children that the office-sitting class (I consider myself to be in this group) could devour, nonstop, on the weekends. For context, Netflix had released its first megahit original series the previous February.

Serial's virality turned true crime into a "new" genre with mass commercial appeal. It also changed the financial forecast for the audio industry overnight.

That same year that *Serial* aired, a podcast outfit called Gimlet Media launched itself with a popular podcast that charted the company's rise, *StartUp*. When I listened to the first episode, I was raking leaves in front of the brownstone where I rented an apartment (Danny and I were, briefly, the small but mighty supers of the building) and literally stepped on the rake—knocking myself in the face like a *Looney Tunes* character. I'd never heard such an intimate portrayal of an active quest—two cofounders of a company documenting, week by week, their successes and failures. The podcast felt alive.

By the following year, Gimlet had brought in $2 million in advertising revenue and closed a round of funding that raised $6 million at a $30 million valuation. The scrappy radio world I'd committed to—with an average annual salary for a midlevel producer, $50,000—was now awash in attention, champagne (I heard), and dough.

Ambitious audio creators saw the success of *Serial* and Gimlet Media and decided to start their own podcast companies. Venture capitalists began pouring cash into the podcast sector, long thought to be *Wait, isn't that just radio?* And WNYC, my employer, wasn't the mightiest audio outfit in town anymore. It looked like I might've missed the wave.

Thus, it came as a surprise to no one but me, when, in January 2015, an old colleague of mine, Andrea, asked if I'd be interested in leaving WNYC to join the new podcast start-up down the block.

At WNYC, I looked at my pay stub and its constantly rolling-over paid time off as the ticket to a long maternity leave in the distant future. I was dug in. I wanted nothing more than to avoid the chaos of my father's career, which had involved riding the wave of the Chicago commodities markets and, when bored, making a series of half-thought-through business investments that went belly-up and left us scrambling. I wanted my future child to have gloves in the winter. That meant I thought my best bet was to stay at the same job for as long as possible and steadily climb its ranks.

But, like most audio producers at the time, I had a nagging suspicion that staying might be just as dangerous as leaving. Public radio was looking like a dinosaur without legs or wings. Also: I was stifled by the narrow parameters of the position. I remembered the observant host of *On the Media* taking me aside to say as much. I was constantly pitching stories, taking on extra assignments, but I kept hitting walls. I also did not have dental insurance.

So when Andrea came knocking, the first question I asked was: Does the company offer dental?

Andrea's employer, *Slate*, did. *Slate* is an online news and culture hub founded in 1996 by Microsoft, during the creation of the dot-com bubble. *Slate* had survived and thrived in the intervening years, and by that time, in 2015, it was one of the handful of websites I looked at first thing on a Monday to stay abreast of the news. *Slate* was also early to podcasting. It already had a podcast chief, an ex-NPR veteran who was keen to grow the audio arm of the business. He wanted to call the audio start-up inside *Slate* Panoply.

I told my boss at WNYC that I had a dental appointment (a small act of spite) and walked the few blocks from WNYC to *Slate*'s then-headquarters in Greenwich Village.

Andrea met me outside. She took me upstairs, and I met my soon-to-be boss and the soon-to-be CEO of the podcast start-up, whose too-bright teeth were the only detail I could later remember about him. Andrea very generously peppered my soon-to-be boss with flattering facts about me, my work ethic, and how I'd won Red Lobster's LobStar of the Week Facebook popularity contest.

They were interviewing other people for the job—a senior producer position—and I truly believe Andrea mentioning my LobStar success was what set me apart from other candidates, like how child actors are encouraged to wear interesting accessories so as to be memorable to casting directors.

"Give a call back to that Red Lobster lady," they may have said after I left the room.

I wrote my soon-to-be boss a thank-you note and also messaged Andrea with appreciation. I went further, asking her for the name and email address of the soon-to-be CEO with the teeth.

Slate made me an offer two days later.

Late on a Friday while that week's episode of *On the Media* was being mixed, I asked the impossibly patient audio engineer if I could use the empty recording room to make a phone call.

"Trouble with my boyfriend," I said.

"Oh!" she said.

You could listen into the recording room with a touch of a button, hence the white lie. The wonderful engineer would never have done that, but I would have done it if the tables were turned.

I got on the phone with my soon-to-be boss and asked for $15,000 above what they were offering, citing the rates of senior producers at other podcasting start-ups. I expected we'd land at $7,500. I got to $10,000! I emerged from the recording room with a smile on my face.

The engineer said, "I guess everything worked out!"

"With what?" I said, panicked.

"Your . . . boyfriend?" she said.

Right, my boyfriend: the almighty dollar.

The official offer letter landed in my inbox on Monday morning. After looking through the dental plans in the benefits package, I went to find my boss. She was in the kitchenette making tea. I asked if we could talk, and she said something along the lines of "Not you, too!"

As the industry boomed, post-*Serial*, WNYC became the obvious place to poach audio producers in the city. Two, then three of the producers on the small *On the Media* team had left by the time I'd gotten my offer. Two of those producers went on to found the show *Reply All*, one of Gimlet's most popular podcasts. Like me, they hadn't planned to ever leave WNYC. But the sudden podcast wave was too good to pass up. Who knew how long it would last and if the money might flow in your direction. At the start, there was more money, upward mobility, and, frankly, more excitement.

"How much are they offering you?" Katya asked, by way of market research more than as a means of counteroffering.

"Seventy thousand. And I'll get dental!" I said, smiling with my beat-up teeth.

"Yeah, we won't be able to come close to that," she said.

"You know, that's a two-level jump from your current position," WNYC's HR rep informed me in my exit interview later.

"I know!" I replied, jaunty.

Really, what tryhard would hear a warning in such a sentence?

I

Job 1

My First Job, Continued

It was February 2004, and I was a junior in high school.

I came home from school with precisely 80 percent of my homework done so that I could watch a specific two-hour block of television before I went to sleep at exactly 9:00 p.m. It was February in Chicago, so it was always cold and dark by 4:00 p.m.

The house seemed empty, but all the lights were on, and my mom's car was in the driveway. I went into the house and immediately smelled it. I saw what I thought was balsamic vinegar all over the kitchen. Glass was everywhere—on the ground, on the counter, in the sink. Also in the sink were cartons and cartons of raw ground meat, just sitting in the open, ready to rot. They smelled like meat rather than grocery freezer, which meant the packages had been out for hours. On the counters was a mixture of specialty grocery items (*Almonds,* I thought, *she must have gone to the fancy Grand Food out of town,* probably trying to avoid being spotted by anyone she knew at the local grocery store), paper bags standing filled with cookies and melting ice cream.

By then my mom was almost completely housebound. Except when she needed more alcohol. And those exceptions were growing. She'd wake up drinking, run out of the wine my dad doled out to her, then try to find a way to get more. So she'd get in her black Nissan and wend her way to a series of different grocery stores, drugstores, and liquor stores. There were rules for my mom, too—how far she would allow herself to drive, the way she wanted to keep up appearances, even though her appearance was "drunk." A different store for each day, five total for the workweek. On the occasions I'd go with her she'd always overexplain what she was doing to the cashier, saying that we were having a party yet again, how hard entertaining was, then buy unnecessary things to keep up with the story. She'd then make some kind of comment about her husband, my dad, to the agreeable but disinterested clerk, who certainly was tired of the overexplanations of the addicts who funded their paycheck.

I knew from the scene in the kitchen that she'd gone on one of these trips alone, and gone early. The meat wouldn't smell so meatish if she'd just gotten back. Nor would the ice cream be melting. She must have started off that morning around a Level 2 on The Chart (nothing higher than that, or else I would've noted her state before I left for school) and would be well on her way to a dangerous Level 4 or an asleep Level 5. An asleep Level 5 could be a blessing and a curse. If she stayed asleep, blessing. If she woke up, curse. I heard nothing.

I walked up the stairs—a three-story rickety wood-and-iron spiral staircase without any barriers between floors, meaning a person could easily trip while climbing up to the second floor and tumble straight down three stories to the basement's concrete floor. When I was young my parents babyproofed the staircase by putting chicken wire around the circular banister at the entrance to the first floor's steps. If you peeked through the chicken wire, it revealed a literal hole in the ground. As a parent now, I'm realizing there's no way us chickens didn't get wired at some point.

The stairs were a sign that this house wasn't meant for children. Maybe wasn't meant for anyone, or at least anyone who didn't want to eventually fall down three flights of stairs and into the basement pit. Those stairs were a symbolic *GET OUT* sign, viewable from the front door.

"We bought the house because of the stairs," my dad had said.

I know at least two of our many cats died by falling into that pit.

The stairs, a metaphor. Anyway . . .

I got to the second floor and saw that the door to my mom's room, which was my older brother's room that she had moved into as soon as he had gone to college, was closed. But there was glass everywhere in the hallway, too. And a frying pan on the ground outside the room. I began realizing that the acid all over the kitchen that I thought was balsamic vinegar was actually some kind of liquor. This discovery meant that, if I had been simultaneously updating my chart while inspecting the second floor, my mom would have hard Level 5 energy. After all, she "only drank wine," which she said piously and often. I put together that she opened a glass liquor bottle by slamming it open with a frying pan—not having the device or the patience to open it and keep it intact. The glass, the frying pan, and the closed door concerned me. This was such a scene—could something have really gone wrong this time?

I moved toward my mother's bedroom and slowly tried to push the door open. It moved, but something was stopping it from opening. I still didn't hear anything. There was give when I pushed, and then pushed harder, and then pushed as hard as I could at—what I soon discovered—was the body on the floor. I got into the room, and the door closed against her weight. The acidic smell was strong. Was she hurt? Was she alive? When I bent down to touch her, to see if she was dead, I first smelled her. She hadn't showered in weeks. A good way to get people to stay away from you. I put my hand underneath her nose to see if she was breathing. Before I could feel her breath, she stirred suddenly, throwing herself to her feet. She leaned against the door, now closed, where she had collapsed. A furious Level 5 on The Chart, and I had no way to leave.

"WHATDAFUCK ARE YOU DOING HERE? YOU'RE A LOSER, LAURA!"

I retreated farther back into her bedroom, which stunk of someone who never left it and of the acidic liquor from downstairs. *Loser* was a favorite word for my mom. Prescient. My dad, a loser for not making enough money. My twin brother, a loser for being too cool in high school. My older brother, a loser for being too into computers. Me, a loser for being a nerd and for, generally, being all up in her business. Or, like that day, a loser for just being alive.

At the time, I weighed around eighty-five pounds. I was five foot two, and the low weight wasn't intentional, but when you're surrounded by the kind of stress that results in charting your mother's mental state every day for your own survival, the pounds just peel off. My mother was taller and bigger than me. And her drive, her fury, added two hundred pounds. She lunged to slap me, and I used the opening to run out the bedroom door.

I grabbed the phone in the hall to dial 911. She grabbed the frying pan on the floor and went to hit me with it. I can't remember what I said on the 911 call. I'm sure it was pretty straightforward: "My mother is very drunk and attacking me and I am worried please come thank you."

As a podcast producer I think about how you'd transcribe the 911 call in a script:

[UNKNOWN RUSTLING]
[UNKNOWN BANGING] [WOMAN SCREAMING]
[GIRL CRYING]

When my mother realized the police were actually coming, she split away from me and the landline. I had finally reached out for help, after years of watching her decline without my dad doing anything about it, but what I did was the greatest betrayal of all. I had snitched. My mom went to her room to freshen up, I suppose. But her secrets were on display, and the police were about to see them.

Two officers arrived. One quickly put me in the back of a squad car and locked the door. I'd been in a police car exactly once and, you guessed it, it was because of the Girl Scouts. The officer recognized me as one of the Scouts. I'd been sitting in the police car for a few minutes when my dad arrived home. He was screaming "What's going on here?!" and waving his arms around in the driveway. He saw me alone in the back of the police car, gave me a passing scowl, and went inside the house. I had said something. I had spilled. This scene, whatever it was, was my fault.

When they brought my mom out, her arms were being held back by the police officers. She was slurring, "Laura, I love you! I'm sorry we couldn't get you the thing you wanted!"

"The thing I wanted" was some item of clothing, I can't remember what. And then I put it together: My parents had told the police that I was mad about not getting something, some material item. Not that there was a dangerous dispute, not that there was a woman so horribly addicted to alcohol that she couldn't function, not that there was a husband coming in to patch things up, not that there was a girl shivering alone in the back of a police car, sure to bring her backpack to finish the remaining 20 percent of her homework. My parents banded together when it came to secrets falling out. And my dad came up with a quick story, one that didn't prevent the arrest but one that cast doubt on me.

"Sorry about your parents' financial troubles," the police officer said to me, as he got in the car.

I arrived at the station and answered some questions. Then I sat and did my math homework. The police officers kept commenting on how skinny and polite I was, a.k.a. an early-aughts Midwestern-child home run. They were nice to me. They brought me milk and candy. The male officer was so embarrassed that he had tears in his eyes when he had to ask me whether I was pregnant. I'm sure I seemed years younger than I was, shivering at a table while my mother was raging on the other side of the police station.

My mother was taken to the hospital. They took her blood alcohol level, and it was very high. No one was surprised. She needed to be there until she sobered up. Then she got to go home.

Someone decided that I would go stay with my fellow Girl Scout Kam for a few days. No one talked about why I was there when I arrived at Kam's house in a police car late at night. I slept on the floor of Kam's room, and her mom made me a sandwich for lunch the next day. I wore the same clothes I'd worn the day before to school—jeans and a slim-cut cream-and-orange raglan sweater.

I don't remember much about those days away from my parents' home. I do remember coming back some nights later to my mom and my dad in the living room, both smug, both drinking. I went to my room. The following weekend they brought me to see a strip mall lawyer who, in his fluorescently lit office, told me that I needed to drop the charges that had been levied on my mom. That I was a liar. That I wouldn't go to college if I didn't do it. He told me to be a big girl, to "just be reasonable."

I was "reasonable" and went in front of a judge and dropped the charges later that week, all the while my parents kept repeating their version of the story.

"Why did you get so upset?" they kept saying.

The only repercussions were a mandated course of family therapy, during which my mom claimed she drank only a glass of wine a day. The Sunday after that therapy session, she told me that she quit drinking. This was on the day of the *Sex and the City* series finale.

"Things won't be like the way they were," she told me, while watching the show.

But she started drinking mouthwash the next day instead.

"I'MNOTDRUNK," she'd slur. Always to me, because I was

always home, always doing my homework and minding her business.

* * *

I went to college. I moved to New York. My mom kept drinking. My mom kept calling, yelling, complaining, and drinking. Every Sunday at 11:00 a.m. EST I'd get the same call, week after week. I stopped keeping up with The Chart—both because I didn't have the data and also because it was too painful to hear her slip away from far away. I felt guilty every day that I wasn't doing my job to help her.

So I continued working at other jobs to help myself.

Job 13

No More Weekends, No More Breath

> **They live like insects, absorbed in petty activities that seem to have nothing to do with any genial aspect of human life.**
>
> Willa Cather, *The Song of the Lark*

Tryhards don't plan to drown. The water rises as they're putting out fires.

I started my new job at Panoply/*Slate* exactly two weeks and one weekend after I gave my notice at WNYC.

They didn't have a desk for me that first day. An apologetic office manager set up a little card table right next to where the podcasts were recorded: a giant, gray, padded box known as a WhisperRoom.

My desk faced directly into the WhisperRoom's only window, meaning I spent my first weeks staring directly in the eyes of whoever was at the host microphone.

The branded-content team sat behind me. These were the folks who created the ads that didn't seem like ads, which were flooding podcasts, digital video, and online articles, paying for the company's existence.

The branded folks were well-dressed sellers with very shiny hair—a type of businessperson I'd never encountered before. They took their clients to SoulCycle for meetings. Several members of the team had desk humidifiers, which made their section look like an enchanted forest. They also talked about how much money they were bringing in. I was scandalized. In public radio you didn't talk about money—in part because it was a nonprofit enterprise but also because a lot of the people who worked there came from it. In for-profit media money was apparently up for conversation. The enchanted forest's ground was littered with gold. Or at least bronze.

My job was to manage the hosts and produce the podcasts that were already in production, and to be involved in the signing and making of new ones.

Andrea, who'd arranged my interview, worked in a different department, so I was building brand-new relationships all around. My direct boss seemed to trust and respect me. This despite my having no experience as a manager and even less business acumen. But who had time for doubts? Not him. Not me. The new podcast network was launching in a matter of weeks.

On the night before we flicked on the proverbial lights, we feverishly uploaded trailers to Apple Podcasts at midnight, racing toward the 3:00 a.m. posting deadline. We could've easily done this uploading work from home, but it didn't occur to me. Going above and beyond in the beginning of a job is always wise; every tryhard knows this.

I stayed even later than my boss, fussing with and checking my spreadsheet twice.

I didn't sleep well that night. Restlessness was running its insistent engine round-the-clock. For the first time in a long time, I was excited. Excited to be part of something new. Excited about the work. Excited to have the feeling of being a full partner in work.

The next day I dutifully showed up to the office on time. It was a cold, windy February morning, and I hadn't fully dried my hair. I remember this detail because the ends were slightly frozen when I took off my hat. I must've looked pretty rough judging by the expressions on the faces from the enchanted forest. My boss was excited by the download numbers and by the press that the network's launch had created. At the end of the day there was a toast—champagne for most, apple juice for some. He made sure to thank me in that toast, despite the fact that I started my work at the company less than a month before.

In short order I was given permission to hire another body for the team, and so recruited a young, exceptional, freelance producer named Henry.

The next months were a blur, during which Henry and I recorded and produced all the podcasts, even as the list of partnerships grew: *New York Magazine, Vox, Vanity Fair, The New York Times,* Food52.

There were unaffiliated journalists signing up, too, ex-members of *Slate* who'd come back to make shows for the network (my favorite being a show called *Podcast for America* hosted by Annie Lowrey, Mark Leibovich, and Alex Wagner; Jon Favreau, a former Obama aide and the founder of Crooked Media and cohost of *Pod Save America,* was a guest on the show and later admitted, or joked, that he came up with *Pod Save America* from *Podcast for America.*).

Bestselling authors were also part of our first waves of launches: Gretchen Rubin and Elizabeth Craft started their show, *Happier with Gretchen Rubin,* with the network; Susan Cain, author of *Quiet: The Power of Introverts in a World That Can't Stop Talking,* had a show. The spring after the launch I got the opportunity to visit Quiet Revolution LLC headquarters, and, let me tell you, it was one of the calmest business operations that I've ever had the pleasure of witnessing.

With the growing suite of shows and the reciprocal revenue, we were able to hire additional freelance producers. I showed the new people the ropes and returned to my laptop, to which I remained glued, day and night, editing podcasts or emailing about podcasts, scheduling or covering for other producers.

All the feedback was positive. There was true momentum, and that was thrilling. But as someone who often confuses excitement with anxiety, I found myself always on edge: waiting for the ding of an email, the swoosh of a text message, the bing of a Slack message.

Danny and I had just moved into our second apartment together, at my insistence. I was forcing a domestic agenda in my new identity as a tenacious, successful worker bee. Among other things, it meant setting down roots—at Panoply—and at our apartment.

"THIS WILL BE THE TABLE WHERE OUR CHILDREN WILL DO THEIR HOMEWORK!" I remember yelling to Danny, outside of Macy's in downtown Brooklyn. We'd gone to the basement to inspect a giant lacquered wooden table I'd seen online. It was later reported that Macy's Brooklyn had a gas leak during the time we were there, but my forcefulness around this table wasn't due to air quality.

One hundred percent acacia, this would be our apartment's first piece of furniture not bought from IKEA or found in the trash. Did the table have chairs? No. It had two benches, also solid acacia wood, which even if we were to buy the table, we would have to buy separately, one day, because we could not afford the table and the "chairs," now. Was delivery free? Of course not.

Danny had no interest in this boondoggle fueled by an

identity crisis I'd been harboring since I was approximately eight years old.

After a day of stony silence over the table dispute, Danny relented. I would buy the table with my new big-girl paycheck. A few weeks later the table came. Danny called me.

"It's gigantic," Danny said.

"Exactly," I responded.

That table is now in pieces in my in-laws' basement in Staten Island. The surface of the table is too rough for art projects, child or adult, too large for any New York real estate that we will ever fill.

But during that era, the Panoply era, the acacia table was where I began taking up space—for my morning before work, every night after work, and every weekend off work, working—even if I had to crawl over it to get to the bathroom.

It was at that table that I received an email with the instructions of the then-chairman of *Slate* to set a meeting with the three hosts of the aforementioned *Podcast for America*. The chairman was personal friends with the talent and wanted to launch the show, as soon as possible.

Back then, the growing competition in podcasting meant everything was always done as soon as possible. Plus, Trump's candidacy for president in 2016 wasn't yet announced, but the man was making noise, and the *Slate* readership was clamoring for more political content about him, about all of it, with the sharp "insideriness" that the hosts were known for.

I set the meeting, over email, at the acacia table, for the next day.

This was a decade before the Pavlok electric shock alarm clock, when mornings meant spackling my face and charging out the door, hair wet, to catch the B train, headed to West Fourth Street. I don't remember if I ate anything that morning. I do remember I had my laptop in my big backpack.

Everyone on that train was doing the same thing: trying to get their ass in their work seat by 9:00 a.m. My home station, Newkirk Plaza, is a relatively early express stop in South Brooklyn. When I usually boarded the train, an hour later, to get to the *Slate* office by ten, there would be enough space on the train for me to hold on to a pole. Perhaps I'd even get a seat. That day, I found myself wedged underneath the armpit of a man wearing natural deodorant, which is to say no deodorant, trying to grip on to the railing above my head. My backpack was wedged between my legs so as not to take up too much room, because I am not a monster.

Between boarding at Newkirk and the next stop at Church Avenue, the sweating began. The water on my hands made it hard to hold on to the now-slick pole above my head.

As the train jolted into Church Avenue, I bent down to readjust my backpack. That's when my vision began to blur. The train continued on, in jerky starts and stops. There was a Q train moving slowly in front of our train.

I felt my head bobbing back and forth without my being

able to control it. The train continued, and my whole body started shaking.

Something was terribly wrong with me physically. Yet I would not be the sick passenger on the train. *You are not the sick passenger, you are not the sick passenger*, I thought, as my vision dimmed, then brightened; as my skin sweated and cooled; as my head bobbed forward and back; as my entire body shook along with the tension of reaching for the pole above my head. I decided I needed to get off the train at the next stop, Prospect Park: an incredibly pleasant-sounding place to have a medical emergency. When the train stopped, I pushed my way through the current of passengers entering and leaving. I was carried along by the crowd to the platform. And then I fainted.

When I came to, I was in the center of the train platform with no one beside me. My backpack was next to me. I was covered in sweat—this detail stuck with me, especially, as I was wearing a white T-shirt and was certainly not competing in a wet T-shirt contest. I didn't know what had happened or why. I sat up and called Danny, telling him I thought I had a stroke. It just so happened that Danny was on the Q train right behind the train I had exited. I sat on the train platform, dazed and alone. To passersby I'm sure I looked hungover or drugged. No one offered to help.

Minutes later Danny appeared and ran toward me. One thing led to another, and we were in a cab to the emergency room.

"I refused to be 'the sick passenger' on the train," I told him, coming down from whatever it was that had just happened.

"I'm proud of you," Danny said.

Danny and I went into the emergency room and were placed in a curtained carrel. The nurse took some blood, some urine, my vitals, and I asked for the wi-fi password. I opened Slack and explained that I would be missing the *Podcast for America* call because I was in the hospital. Initially no one responded.

I started checking my email, going about my various comfort corporate routines I'd imposed upon myself. We sat on the bed in the emergency room, me on my laptop, Danny fearfully sitting with his hands in his lap. That's when I received a Slack message from a colleague: "The meeting didn't happen because you didn't show up. By the way, you never should have set it for a Monday morning."

Rage, to me, feels like a boiling warmth that comes from my feet, spreads through every vein, and blasts into my head. "But," I said out loud to myself and, presumably, to Danny, who was also sitting there, "I was told to set the meeting for this morning, Monday morning."

I returned the message with the line that should get you out of anything and everything: "I'm sorry. I'm in the hospital." I wish I had the presence of mind to just say, "I am in hospital," so the grammar would be both confusing (*Is she British?!*) or potentially alarming (*She can't write in full sentences*).

I was so angry about the Slack message that my hair could've been on fire. The rage washed away the reason I was in the hospital in the first place. Then the doctor came in and closed the curtain.

Shit, I thought.

Danny sat up straight.

"It seems like you had a panic attack," the doctor said.

"A panic attack?" I'd read enough memoirs to know that having panic attacks was both a rite of passage and a pretty bad excuse for my work purposes.

"Nothing came back out of range. Remember to drink water and eat in the morning," the doctor finished.

Thank-yous were exchanged. Danny and I left to get my discharge paperwork.

"Well, I didn't die," I said, looking at my phone on Fourth Avenue in Brooklyn.

"When the doctor closed the curtain, I thought he was going to say you were pregnant," Danny said.

"Pregnant? No. Wait. How did you feel about that?"

"Happy."

* * *

We got back to the apartment. I set up my laptop at my wooden monstrosity to catch up on emails. No one had responded to my note about not making the meeting, other than the coworker who chided me for setting the meeting for a Monday morning.

I was still angry, but the anger faded as I went back to the hamster wheel. A day of emails turned to a night of emails. I put on a clay face mask to combat my adult acne. I washed off the mask and went to sleep.

I got to work the next day, and my colleague—who I'll call Moel Jeyer—took me aside.

"We really have to do something about this," he said.

"About what?" I said.

He told me the way I was working wasn't healthy for me. That I needed more support. I said I was "fine," which is the universal descriptor for someone who is, in fact, not "fine."

Keeping budgets low and my productivity high was my new definition of doing the best work I possibly could be doing. My literal sweat, the various humors removed from my body in the ER the day before, were proof that I was committed, that I was a success and suited to the work.

I look back on that conversation, on Moel Jeyer's kindness, often. This wasn't his first rodeo, and he took time out to tell me—someone clinging hard to the belly of a bucking horse—that it didn't need to be this way. And Moel was not wrong. But I couldn't hear him then.

The pace continued, and I happily obliged. We did a hiring spree. I built an entire editorial and branded-content team in New York. I got married on Thursday, October 15. We took pictures in the parking lot of Staten Island Borough Hall. The next day I got fitted for Invisalign braces (the high school dream borne out!) and went on to work to produce two pilots for the author of (and creator of the term) *#Girlboss* herself: Sophia Amoruso.

Sophia sent me the classiest bouquet of flowers I've ever received. My teeth pulsed underneath my new aligners.

I was succeeding!

I'd soon have teeth as straight and white as the CEO's. Working the day after my wedding: that was commitment that nobody could deny.

卌 卌 ||||

Job 14

The Woman Who Lived in an Org Chart

> **The existing system is the game of business. The landscape which has been contoured out of a military-sports subsoil is the territory of play, the game board.**
>
> Betty Lehan Harragan, *Games Mother Never Taught You*

If you've browsed podcasts (not to mention bookstores, speaking series, or *The New Yorker*), you are aware of Malcolm Gladwell. The man is famous. He popularized the idea that if you focus your attention sincerely on doing or learning something for ten thousand hours, you could be an expert. That idea of his, in particular, is an inescapable meme. And, inescapable to me. If you try hard enough, engrave your brain enough with the neural wiring needed to get something done, you can do it. If you have the will.

When Gladwell walked through Panoply's doors to pitch his podcast *Revisionist History*, in 2016, I was literally quaking in my boots (which, to fit with the style of the time, were somehow both clogs and ankle boots; they were also heavy and loud, incapable of emitting anything but a stomp).

I built Gladwell's first audio team from scratch: I found a freelance lead producer/showrunner, an editor, a composer, a mix engineer, and got access to a recording studio that was not the unglamourous WhisperRoom (which, not too long before his visit, I had needed to have professionally disinfected after all of its microphones were exposed to the mumps). All of this on a minuscule budget.

Gladwell didn't seem much interested in collaboration, which worried me a little. I knew he was smart and, like most writers, a lone wolf, but audio was a different medium than he was used to. So as recording day approached, I organized a table read: basically, a giant meeting in which the host reads aloud the script he's written.

This is an excellent trick for self-revelation. Gladwell started reading his first script to the room and immediately realized something was wrong.

He sounded like he was reading a *New Yorker* article. A very well-written, Malcolm Gladwell–ian essay, but a dry lecture at best. There were no sensory details or conversational tics. It lacked the liveliness—the life, really—that a good podcast has. I can't recall exactly what he said after, but it was something like "This isn't working."

To which I likely responded, "Yeah."

The podcast team I'd assembled raised its nose in unison, like a collection of in sync pointer dogs, and followed him off to fix the script. Though he was the leader of the pack, he was no longer a lone wolf.

From that day on, the podcast team was a well-oiled machine. *Revisionist History* is still producing new episodes, as of the printing of this book.

A few days after the table read I got an email from my boss as I was on my way into the office. Would I come to the "brass" meeting—a meeting of the leadership of the company?

"Sure," I responded, wiping doughnut glaze off my hands.

This meeting included my boss, who'd been promoted to chief creative officer; the man with the blinding teeth, who was now officially the chief executive officer; the chief revenue officer, who was head of the enchanted forest; the president of *Slate*; and the technical lead.

These were all the company's main men. They had their own brass LISTSERV. And now I was being added to it, the leadership team, me. I'd been so busy doing and making from my gigantic Macy's farm table, I hadn't even thought to ask to join.

The joy sat with me for about thirty seconds. Because a

tryhard can set a new goal only after one is achieved. I sat in those weekly meetings hearing detailed financial updates, context for short-term goals, and plans for longer-term ones. I finally got a look into the guts of the operation.

We moved to a new office in downtown Brooklyn. This helped me, personally, since it shortened my commute and subway trains were the source of pesky panic aftershocks.

I still found myself with the familiar shaky-sweaties as soon as the B train went underground after the Prospect Park stop. Not because of a flashback from the first panic attack, I realized, but because my cell phone lost service when the train went underground.

What if someone sent me a work email, a Slack, or a text message to which I couldn't immediately reply? As soon as the train emerged onto the Manhattan Bridge, my cell service returned and so did my bodily sanity.

By that point I'd finally gotten into talk therapy, to deal with the train panic attacks. (Reader: I am still in therapy, almost ten years later, and let me tell you what—there was more than just the train to discuss.)

Despite my first attempts to gain more insight into my work obsession in therapy, the twenty-four-hour clock had almost no meaning in my life. I worked no matter the hour. Every weekday I returned home around 7:00 p.m. to continue work at my tree slab. The weekends were fair game, too. Danny had started complaining about me never being available to do, well, anything. I was either working or sleeping. I'd lost ten pounds from anxiety, and my hair had started falling out.

But, bright spot: The new office was delightfully large and airy, with three full podcast studios—with lights, windows, everything—and a giant television in the café area!

Best of all, the WhisperRoom was gone. I like to imagine it in a nice home, maybe the basement of some marketing executive in Paramus, New Jersey, who loves the sound of his own voice. And don't we all?!

We used every last one of our new studios. At all hours. The soundboards might as well have had smoke pouring out of them.

One evening, I was sitting in on a recording for a podcast when I heard what sounded to me like a series of corpses being thrown on the floor, as their enormous, grunting murderers picked them up and chucked them—over and over. The slams and grunts were bleeding into the recording.

I stormed down the hallway to our neighbors on the floor: Tough Mudder, a company that then primarily organized mud runs with fire obstacles in the tristate area. *Slate* had sublet its floor from Tough Mudder—a hilariously unnatural pairing—and our recording studio walls abutted Tough Mudder's "experiment room"—whatever that was. I was about to find out.

"Will you be doing this for long?" I asked primly, with my Invisalign fangs.

"Yeah. We're testing out a new course," said Andre the Giant.

I'm not sure he saw the shrimp at his feet, at first.

"What's with the loud thumping?" I pressed. I didn't mention the grunts because I'm a professional.

"The heaviest sandbags on the market."

And scene.

The next day, the legal counsel, and the person who knew the details of the Tough Mudder lease, pulled me aside.

"Did something happen here last night?"

"We recorded a podcast?" I said tentatively.

"I'm asking because one of the managers from Tough Mudder came down here this morning asking about an 'angry blond woman.' Was that you? Because Tough Mudder can do whatever it wants, after hours. It's their space."

I pulled a strand of my hair in front of my face: not blond. But, I took the compliment.

Angry, yes, very very angry, growing more so.

No one tells a tryhard member of the *brass* to stand down when she is clearly hustling at all hours, well beyond anyone's expectations, for the advancement of her company!

But this lawyer just had. And she was now a member of the brass, too.

I don't know what I said in reply. Possibly I tucked in my lips and said nothing. I would like to think I had a shred of self-preserving instinct left by then. But that would be very generous of present me to believe in past me.

Did it cross my mind that I was, perhaps, working too hard in the wrong directions? That I was spending my weeknights nursing grudges on strongmen who had every legal right to throw the heaviest sandbags on the floor for any reason? That I was, physically, geared up to fight with a lawyer for my right to break the rules? For the first time, yes, it did!

Did I blame Panoply for this newfound aggression, instead of myself? Absolutely!

This was a tryhard revelation for me. Instead of blaming myself for "bad behavior"—meaning *any* type of constructive feedback, because at this point in my life, such feedback equated to I was doing something wrong—I directed my ire outward. Of course, I wasn't yet able to express these thoughts to the lawyer. That would come later. But I emerged from my Tough Mudder dustup as their brand would hope: with a new type of ferocity toward work.

* * *

Listening to podcasts, or something like podcasts, on my little portable CD player in the children's library in Glencoe, Illinois, had been one of my greatest escapes when I was young. But during this time at Panoply, I couldn't bring myself to listen to podcasts outside of the ones I was producing. My free time—meaning, when I walked from the train to my desk, or from the train to my home-desk slab—was now spent listening to nothing. I'd put my headphones on out of habit and not turn anything on, to chug through a muted version of the world around me. I created a buffer from myself and the reality around me because I couldn't quite face it.

There was one exception: *Bitch Sesh*, a *Real Housewives* breakdown podcast.

Despite centering my entire life around work, I still found time to comfort myself, occasionally, by watching women scream at each other on *The Real Housewives* when I brushed my teeth or took a shower, on my phone's tiny screen. It was like watching the inside of my own brain, the darkest corners. I discovered *Bitch Sesh* about twenty episodes in, which meant I had the unique pleasure of listening through a back catalog.

One of their podcast ads was for pills made of actual shark that were meant to help with hair growth. I bought them, with their show's unique promo code, and took them dutifully. The pills tasted like shark: fishy with a bloody, coppery aftertaste. My hair did grow back in soft, ducky tufts.

I was managing twenty people and perhaps forty podcasts. If someone had a question, they went to me—hence all the emails.

There's this old management chestnut called "the Bus Factor." If one person were to get hit by a bus, would that company be able to continue operating without said dead bus person (RIP)? At that time, I was the person most vulnerable to buses. I raised this problem with my boss. I got up the courage to tell him that I thought I deserved a promotion and that my role needed to be split into a creative and an operational role. I told him I wanted the creative role.

My boss was incredibly well-meaning. But something

about that conversation didn't quite land with him. A week later, a man unknown to everyone but the chairman of *Slate* came into the office. He was from England (fancy!). My boss went around introducing him to everyone. At the end of the day my boss called me into the office.

"What did you think of [the British man]?"

"He seems fine," I said.

"Great. Should I write to everyone letting them know about their new boss?"

I thought, *What the actual fuck?* At no point was this British man mentioned as the new head of content, to me at least, by my boss. Where was this coming from? Why would this stranger blow into town and suddenly outrank all the work I'd done building the entire editorial side of the company? Was this some kind of favoritism happening at the highest level of the company—maybe not in the brass meetings, but perhaps the platinum ones (if they existed)? Something had gotten lost in corporate translation. I told my boss to hold off on that announcement and left his office.

My boss seemed to think I'd be thrilled to learn from this British hotshot. I may not have been British, but I was determined to be The Hotshot.

Cue the angriest woman in the world furiously leaving the office and stomping to Chipotle. I can still hear my clog boots on the ground, feel the shin splints that would've resulted from that level of angry stomping every day. This perfectly fine British person was *not* to be everyone's boss. I was everyone's boss. I got a giant burrito, returned home to my slab, and began making an organizational chart (which did not yet exist at Panoply) without so much as taking off my raincoat.

I gave myself a new title, one that felt appropriate to my work: vice president of content.

The next day I reached out to the CEO, based in DC, the man of very white teeth and increasing power. He asked to see my new org chart, then requested a call. I went into one of the phone booths scattered across the newsroom. They were booths meant for privacy when making calls to sources. In practice I found those booths were more often used to take personal calls that resulted in people crying or to do job interviews.

"I'm going to help you with this," the CEO said.

"Wow, thank you," I said.

"Let me take a look at the new org chart. Then I'll come to New York next week, and we'll talk with your boss."

A week passed by. I changed Invisalign retainers. I felt forward momentum. On the day of the meeting with the CEO and my boss, my teeth hurt. I was about to get what I determined was my due, and I was about to have the straightest damn teeth in the world.

In the meeting I reshared the org chart. My boss studied it and said, "Looks good to me."

The cool douse of relief.

"Wait a second, a vice president role? I don't think that makes sense," the CEO said, pointing at the chart.

I don't say this lightly: but, truly, what a bastard. The CEO, who had offered to help me, who had seen my plan, had set me up. That man was, once again, just a set of teeth to me. The first and only time I've maligned teeth. I didn't get a promotion or any more clarity from that meeting. But I did get even angrier.

The first woman in the brass meeting with a group of men; the first employee of the company who started nearly all the podcasts; the person who, for some reason, ended up selling the ad space on the first season of Malcolm Gladwell's *Revisionist History* the day before the show launched; the person who devoted her life to this job to show how competent she could be; the most productive member of the team? "A vice president role? I don't think that makes sense."

I went home that day and applied a Bioré strip I'd been saving since 2009. I needed to see some real progress in the form of whatever the hell was about to be ripped off my face. Danny came home, surprised not to see me at my slab, and asked what happened.

I told him. I also told him I was going to find a new job.

I reached out to the content head of the podcast company that made *Bitch Sesh*. I called the show what it is: a revelation. Their executive producer of podcast development—the person charged with making new shows—had recently left. Would I like to talk about the job? the content head asked.

A week passed, and I was back at the orthodontist. I felt old and at home with the toothy, insolent teens in that waiting room.

My beloved orthodontist, Kenneth Cooperman, called me in. We were near the end of my treatments, with only "refinements" left to do. Did I need a final course of refinement aligners?

No, I did not.

"Amazing job. You're done," Dr. Cooperman said.

Everything at that time sounded like a psychic message.

Feeling generally out of control, drunk with powerlessness around leaving Panoply, I determined it was time for me to shoot my shot.

"I noticed there's a Patient of the Month sign. Can I be on it?" I asked.

Dr. Cooperman paused.

"That's an award for children," he said, smiling stiffly, and very quickly exited the room.

I went to a series of job interviews for a role at the other podcast company. Two days before my thirtieth birthday, the offer letter came in.

As was my practice, I examined the salary (I negotiated a signing bonus this time), the dental, and the benefits package. I then knocked on my boss's door.

I sat down and told him that I would be leaving the company for another job and that I'd like to discuss timing. I could give two, three, four weeks' notice—whatever worked best for everyone.

My boss looked at me blankly. I don't remember what he said, but I remember how I felt: like I joyfully jumped off a ship but didn't know how to swim and now was sinking. I went back to my desk. He stormed out of his office and left for the day.

The next day, I turned thirty and got drug tested for my new job. Despite literally never taking an illicit drug in my life, I was worried I'd fail the test due to the SSRI I was on. I called my psychiatrist and left him a message. "This is urgent!" I said. He returned the call, calmly, informing me that Lexapro was not an illegal substance and I had nothing to worry about. My extreme concern about this easily googleable fact might have suggested to him that I needed to take more of it.

Drug test done, I went to the old podcast factory that I was leaving. The CEO was sitting with my boss in his office. He had come back in from DC. They both summoned me. That day would be my last day, they said. Because of my boss's door slam the day before, I figured that might happen. I'd prepared a handoff memo the previous night. But there was more.

"We are calling an all-hands meeting," the CEO said.

"Okay," I said.

"You're to tell everyone you're leaving the company for

personal reasons and that you have great faith in the company," he said.

"Okay," I said. Standing before the CEO and my boss felt remarkably like standing before my mother and father in that moment.

"And you're going to sign this paper now. This paper says we are taking all of your phantom equity in the company. You're going to a competitor," he said.

Quick tip: Never sign anything without having a lawyer read it. The CEO had given me the impression that if I didn't sign it, I wouldn't have access to the month of health insurance I was worried I'd lose, since I'd be beginning my new job a month later. He handed me a pen. And, ever the sucker for the maintenance and retention of health benefits, I signed it.

Since I was the first employee at Panoply, I had a larger share in the company than every other employee, except for everyone else who already worked at *Slate* and made up the original brass meetings. I didn't think about what I was giving up with this piece of paper. I was too consumed, suddenly, with what I was giving up in leaving this job—a job that I thought made me valuable—skilled, devoted, marketable, and on an upward trajectory.

What that job actually made me was unvaluable—meaning I was needed, but only in the capacity I held at Panoply. I wasn't seen as a growing figure at the company. I was a dependable database, a replicable cog who'd always show up (except when in the hospital), who'd share my screen with all the documents I made, who'd pour water for everyone at the meetings. I was meant to stay in my place, provide my services, and be grateful to do just that.

The CEO called the all-hands meeting in the conference room. The previous year on my birthday the producers organized what my first boss at WNYC would call "a cake event." What a wonderful phrase. There was an ice cream cake and there were little toasts, and it was very nice. Since many of the producers knew I was turning thirty that day, they later told me they thought I was being surprised in the conference room.

I went into the room as instructed. I sat next to my boss and across from the CEO. The room was full of about twenty people, with ten more joining over Zoom.

"I believe Laura has some things to say," the CEO said.

"I'm leaving the company. For personal reasons," I said.

Now, at this point, I started to cry. An amazing human reaction that I wish didn't exist about 75 percent of the time it happens. Particularly the 25 percent of the time in which I've recently gotten eyelash extensions. I was in that 25 percent period.

"I have great faith in the company's success," I choked out.

The room, silent. The faces on Zoom, shocked.

"Laura will be here until the end of the day," the CEO said.

After a minute everyone started filing out of the room. No questions were solicited.

When I passed the CEO at the door, he said, "I think it's time for you to leave, Laura."

I put a Post-it note with my computer password on my laptop. What true humiliation . . . to reveal what configuration of your cats' names and the number 69 make up your work computer's password. I printed it out and placed my exit memo on my boss's desk.

Producers started coming up to me with small gifts they'd gotten me for my birthday. Silly cards. Cat toys. A glass six-pack of artisanal ginger ale.

I walked out of the office and to the uptown R train. What the hell was I supposed to do without work? What the hell did I just sign? Where was I going? I threw the ginger ale in a trash can, the sound of shattered glass echoing in the empty subway station.

All that equity I signed away? Something they never asked another employee to do again, whether going to a competing company or not, by the way. That company went on to be sold for $235 million.

The day the acquisition news broke, I slammed my laptop shut (spoiler: I was at a different job by then) and nearly threw it across the room like a Frisbee. I did the math: If I'd been able to keep my equity, I would've probably made close to one million dollars in the transaction. If I had only kept my mouth shut, been content with where I was, I could buy an apartment—not to flip but to live in until I died in it, thereby making it a stigmatized property (this is a dream of mine).

And then I remembered a personal motto, one that should be tattooed on my body, that I think and/or say so often: *Money isn't real until it clears your bank account.* And I wouldn't have been me if I had stayed at that job, miserable and green from the nausea that comes with constant sleep deprivation.

Dear reader, if you find yourself at a start-up your compensation may include equity (often in lieu of an appropriate salary). If you're able to swing it, then *sick*. Hold on to that paper, that lottery ticket. But, if you're like most of us, the dream of riches will never come to bear. With that in mind, here are some tips for working at a start-up:

1. Make sure your base salary covers your base expenses. Don't expect a bonus to make you whole. Despite what anyone during the onboarding process says, bonuses are never guaranteed, especially with a start-up.

2. Give as much as you get. One time I was complimented on a staff call for working all night on a heavily manual task. Instead of, say, a spot bonus, I was given twelve mini cupcakes that I ate over the course of six hours.

3. Keep track of your tasks and document them. In start-ups you'll often be asked to do at least two people's jobs. If the company succeeds, use that documentation to push for another job opening. Don't stake your identity on being the person who does everyone's work for them.

4. Morale may be low due to the, generally, small amount of people doing a lot of work. This will result in forced fun team-building morale events. Going to a mandatory event at a Ping-Pong bar on a Tuesday night doesn't replace money. By the by, I have been forced into planning and then attending a Ping-Pong bar party as a mandatory morale booster. When I went running after a Ping-Pong ball, I found myself at Malcolm Gladwell's and one of the company's bigwig's feet. When I looked up, mortified, the bigwig said, "Laura, this is *luxury* Ping-Pong. They'll get the ball for you." I haven't picked up a paddle since.

5. If you wear mascara, I suggest you develop the controversial ability to apply it while on public transit. You will be getting less sleep than expected and will always be on the verge of being late to work. Find a mirror you can balance on your knees so you can steady your non-dominant hand as your dominant brushes on the lash lacquer. This will provide extra stability.

Job 15

Anger Management

Most women don't have careers, they have jobs. They're told they have careers, because that suits the employers. "Career" is such an artificial concept. It's just people up there making money out of people down here, I'm afraid.

Fay Weldon, author and essayist

Leaving Panoply and starting a job at a different podcast company felt like an immediate exhale. Both a relief and a deflation. At the new job, I rode the train home from the offices in Midtown while the sun was still out. I got home and rested. I became incredibly skilled at playing the Nintendo game *Overcooked!*—a game meant for two people—as a single player. It's a cooking time-management game in which you inhabit cartoon chefs dealing with increasingly chaotic cooking scenarios and themes (haunted castles, lava, rivers, zombies). Night after night, I'd focus my attention on switching my controller from one cartoon chef to the other, at first to complete the entire game on my own. And then to continually beat my own records. I kept a notebook of the levels I needed to perfect.

"This game is just stressful for me to watch," Danny said, returning to reading something on his iPad.

At my new job I wasn't expected to respond to emails off-hours. In fact, I once sent a semi-time-sensitive email to my boss on a weekend, and he responded by telling me to get offline and we'd deal with it on Monday.

And yet, as my devotion to *Overcooked!* might suggest, I still had the itchy determination to win a game against myself. And it was only a matter of time before that spilled into my working life.

In 2017 I was the dedicated executive producer at a podcast company, charged with developing all the company's new shows. These shows were both originals from the company, plus producing new shows for some big hosts, clients, who signed ad deals with the company.

I determined that having a handle on the deal flow—that is, knowing about prospective projects and the speed at which contracts closed—would be key to my success at the company. So I made friends with the company's lawyer, who held the keys to that particular castle. Several people who'd worked with him for a while warned me against this allegiance, generally with various vague noises such as *ugh* and *bleh* when his name came up. These warnings, as usual at that time, didn't stop me from barreling forward.

My collegial friendliness with the lawyer immediately helped. He explained the way the green light meeting worked, he showed me a spreadsheet called the "deal-o-matic," which used audience projections (based on marketing spends), advertising revenue (based on the assumed listener demographic), and production costs (what it would cost my team to make a show), to determine which projects would be green-lit.

I brought a project to him, a show I wanted to make about Multilevel Marketing schemes. Multilevel Marketing (MLM) occurs when companies sell a product, yes, but generally they make the real money by recruiting people to sell the product to *other* would-be sellers underneath them, known as their "downlines." The proceeds from the downlines trickled up to the top of the pyramid-shaped organizational structure. Some MLMs are legitimate, sure. Above board MLMs sell a product with value that's meant to turn profits for all involved. But the ones I'd seen explode across my corner of the internet were pyramid schemes. I wanted to make an original true-crime franchise about business scams, which was, then, a novel idea. The show would eventually go on to be called *The Dream*.

The lawyer and I worked together to make the "deal-o-matic" data show more profit than loss for *The Dream*. To make that happen, I said, choking back something that tasted like pride in the green light meeting, I said, "We can market it as a business show for ladies. Um, like, *lady business*."

"Lady business!" the head of sales hooted, pleased. Selling products to women and selling products in the business space were, and still are, two lucrative ad opportunities in podcasting.

"Yes . . . lady business," I said.

The project was green-lit then and there.

The lawyer helped get the project over the line. I was thankful for this. After, he expected me to help him. Fair enough. But it quickly became apparent that what he wanted was carte blanche to create new podcasts of his own for talent he signed to the network, via me, the person who was formally charged with creating new podcasts. He'd Slack me endlessly—talking about various small-time celebrities he met with who needed a show (think anyone who was in a two-season sitcom in the late nineties or early aughts); agents or managers he wanted to curry favor with by commissioning a show for one of their clients; once, he told me he'd already agreed to produce a pilot for the Democratic National Committee (the lawyer had political aspirations). His aboveboard favor to me turned into a quid pro quo that spun out of control.

He brought these ideas to the green light meeting, citing

my implicit blessing of the content, along with financials he determined himself. These projects would then be assigned to my team to produce and would also take up my budget. I brought this concern to my boss.

"Ah, yes, [the lawyer]. He's a regular Cecil B. DeMille of podcasts," my boss said, throwing his hands up.

And that's where the conversation ended. The lawyer predated my boss and was close with the CEO. My sense was my boss didn't want to rock the boat.

Suddenly, my producers were pulled into these confusing projects for outside hosts. And, sure enough, when the shows started production, the lawyer showed up on every call, yessing the talent to death and agreeing to all their ideas. This neutered the producers from having any ability to properly produce the shows and made the producers wonder what the hell I was doing "blessing" these ideas.

This happened a handful of times before I realized what was going on: The lawyer wanted my job. And, because he had done me a series of favors by showing me how the deals got done and by helping push through *The Dream*, he figured he might as well take over.

Now I had a grudge. One that I was nurturing into a full-blown storm of hatred that I kept to myself . . . mostly. Though soon enough, one night I exited an evening Orangetheory class, checked my email, received one with production instructions from the lawyer, and fired off an absolutely apoplectic response while fuming on Flatbush Avenue.

There was the anger. Part of my fuel. Perhaps if I had spoken up and allowed the steam to escape, I wouldn't blow my lid. Again.

The next shot opens on our hero sitting in a conference room of a certain talent agency known by its three-letter acronym (all talent agencies seem to have three-letter acronyms, so this is giving away nothing, but boy do I feel like Nikki Finke writing that last sentence). I should note that this is not one of the premier conference rooms—the ones with the frosted glass through which you can glimpse the aura of celebrity, though their anonymity remains intact. Those boardrooms often have separate entrances and exits away from the hoi polloi office workers. The conference room I am sitting in stands right off the reception area and next to the bathrooms. No frosted windows. No glamour. Only the public entrance. Only the public exit.

This is Los Angeles, which is not my home turf. Really, neither is New York, which I have been borrowing since college graduation, but at least I am at home there; its many forms of public transportation make me powerful in a world where I cannot drive. When in LA, I often try to walk places that shouldn't be walked to, which leaves me taking phone calls in parking lots or walking along the side of too-busy roads like a scared teacup Maltese in need of grooming. Needless to say, there's a chance I did not feel I had the upper hand in the lesser conference room.

I'm sitting across from three men—a talent agent and two

colleagues from the podcast company where I worked after Panoply: the lawyer who I will not name because he's a lawyer, and a fellow producer, who I'll call Ted, who I've invited for moral support and who has agreed to come for the free sandwiches.

I'm the only woman in the room. This was common. I've recently poured everyone water. I am technically tied for the most "senior" person in the room, but I am accustomed to being the default water pourer.

Tip: Never pour water for everyone in the conference room unless it's your actual job to do so.

I've flown across the country to the three-letter talent agency to meet the cohosts of a very popular podcast in a very popular genre. For months I've been brainstorming ideas—by phone—with these popular podcast cohosts, to help them build more shows, and I'm keen to meet them in person for the first time, to convey my dedication to their cause.

My producers and I love the podcast. In particular we love the cohosts of this very popular podcast in a very popular genre who I am meeting today. We've done at least a dozen calls with them. The popular cohosts seem at times confused, mysteriously angry, and then silent on these calls, but we are persisting. Something isn't quite right, but we will solve it. I am optimistic, verging on delusional. I spend weekends working through pitch decks for them. I create spreadsheets explaining what my producers and I can offer their shows. I figure that, with work, whatever tension that seems to be brewing would resolve. Creative partnerships don't materialize overnight.

Then, I'm summoned to LA. The handler of the very popular cohosts gives no reason for the invite.

Whenever anyone tells you to come to Los Angeles without telling you why you need to come to Los Angeles, it's a bad sign. No one will be giving you a check if they tell you to come meet them in LA without a reason.

But I'm getting ahead of myself.

Back in the lesser conference room, the popular cohosts have yet to arrive. Their agent, the podcast company's lawyer, Ted, and I wait. The agent and lawyer tap their impatient fingers on the table. Then the podcast company's lawyer chirps up, says something about my being brought out to LA to be "auditioned."

"Excuse me? Auditioned for what?" I ask.

"To see if you've got *it*," the lawyer says.

"Got . . . *what*?" I say.

The two empty seats next to me seem to groan now with the waiting. As the minutes tick by, the agent across the table grows twitchy.

Note to past self from current self: If an agent is nervous, you should be nervous.

When the very popular cohosts finally arrive, they blast through the glass conference room doors like a cold front. Imagine all the following being said with the hard, fast bang of hailstones hitting a windshield:

"Why haven't we gotten what we were told we would get?"

I think, *What exactly were they supposed to get?* I am confused, but I've watched enough reality television to be able to read the room during the conflict. On one side of the table, two women (the talent) yelling at one confused woman (yours truly). If this scene were scored, my silence would be punctuated with the squeal of a high-pitched violin, waiting for me to speak.

The violin still squealing in my silence, on the other side of the table, the three men (the suits) are silent. One, my producer friend, is eating a sandwich, equally confused (the reality TV camera would've skipped his eating). The camera on my boring reality show would've panned over and zoomed into the other two men, the podcast company's lawyer and the agent, silently staring at me. Waiting for me to say something to, I quickly realize, take a fall for the hosts' (their clients') unhappiness.

"What the contract said we would get?" they continue. "You're in breach!"

Perhaps "you're in breach" should be in the title of this book, but *I am not a lawyer*. At the podcast company I never saw so much as the contract we made with freelance producers for temporary work. Who did see, negotiate, and draw up those contracts, especially for talent like these very popular podcast cohosts? The podcast company's lawyer and their agent, both of whom continue staring at me, seeing how I will respond.

I freeze still silent. The cohosts continue.

"Why are we waiting around for anything to happen? This deal is worth millions, and this is amateur hour. This is podcasting! We are from *television*," they say.

They are talking fast and loudly. They are angry. The agent starts looking down at the shiny table. The lawyer, too. Ted, my plus-one, is still eating a sandwich. I, having fully taken the temperature of the room, am shivering.

The cohosts of the very popular podcast aren't angry at everyone in the room. They are angry at me. They are looking directly and only at me as they perform their tirade. Somewhere along the line, I realize the podcast company's lawyer or their agent blamed me when whatever deal they made with the hosts about making new shows went sideways. I look for something to hold on to and can only see the handle of the water jug.

Here is what I'm not aware of but will become aware of in the next several hours: Approximately six months before this meeting, the two very popular cohosts signed a deal with the podcast company—via the company's lawyer and their agent—for eight figures. A podcast deal that, back then, was one of the biggest ever.

Buried in this millions-of-dollars contract was a little line that required the very popular cohosts to produce a half-dozen podcasts. I did not know this, but the lawyer did. The lawyer fancied himself a producer, after all—of television, of films, of internet videos, of podcasts. A regular Cecil B. DeMille, per my boss. He tried to develop the shows himself. When he failed to do so, the hosts became angry, and the lawyer punted the problem to lil ole me, who knew nothing of the backstory.

So the tension I sensed on the phone during all those meetings the month before? It was all leading up to this scene in the lesser conference room.

"Who do you think you are?" one of the cohosts says, a phrase that hits a particular tenderness.

To avoid crying I am doing the thing I heard a fellow LA icon, Lisa Vanderpump, tell her SURvers: "Breathe through your nose, darling." My nostrils are definitely flaring.

"And clearly," one cohost yells, "you're angry. Why are you angry?"

I try to protect my anger at all costs. It is mine, my fuel. But point it out? That is it. The switch.

Want to turn a cold talent agency boardroom hot? Start crying. Just bawling across the table from three people, two of whom hoped this would happen so they'd stop receiving angry phone calls from the talent, and the last one missing his second sandwich.

"Why are you crying?"

"I'm crying," I say, "because I've disappointed you."

A survival half apology. Backed into a corner, I know I can't throw back blame to the two men. This isn't a game I am going to win in the moment, nor do I fully understand, yet, how I've been duped: The lawyer kept the talent on the hook for months, screwed up the relationship in the process, and then passed the problem to me. I swallow my anger like gum. A problem I'll save for indigestion later.

The talent says nothing at my tears.

The meeting ends shortly, and saltily, thereafter. The talent leaves the conference room first, shaking their agent's hand. Once the coast is clear, the lawyer and my producer friend shake the outstretched hand of the agent. The agent doesn't offer his hand for me to shake. Then, we leave the building.

It is raining in LA that day. We—the lawyer, my producer friend, and I—stand outside the three-letter agency and wait for a cab. The lawyer, now my official nemesis, swats away individual raindrops from his head, as if that sort of deflection were actually possible. His hair is wet and so is his entire arm.

"Yeah, we gotta take you off the project," he says.

It would be easier to make me just disappear than try to explain the nuances of not sharing the contract details with me, but suffice it to say, the lawyer really screwed me over.

"No shit," I say.

* * *

I immediately, furiously ditch work and find myself at the mall with two friends who've moved from New York to LA to be, unironically, near malls.

"WHAT THE ACTUAL FUCK?" I howl while standing in front of a McDonald's.

One of the two friends, Rachel, urges me to keep walking.

"When we first moved here, we signed up for the Planet Fitness over there." She points to a hole in the ground.

"It's a hole in the ground?" I say.

"Yeah, it never opened," Rachel's partner, Jesse, says.

We stand there in silence, gazing at the metaphor. To this day, thinking of signing up for a gym that's a literal pit in the ground still calms me down.

"You gotta just write an email to the cohosts of the very popular podcast in a very popular genre," Rachel says. Easy for a screenwriter.

"SAYING WHAT?"

"You cried. It sucks. Whatever. But if you really want to save face, just put yourself on their side. That's how you'll win them over," Rachel says.

To everyone's relief, I leave the mall. The barometric pressure lowers. Credit card machines start working again. Perhaps the Planet Fitness pit starts filling in with dirt and gym equipment. I climb into a cab and return to my hotel with a bag full of hamburgers and a plan.

I write the cohosts an email. I do not blame anything on anyone—including myself. I tell them the truth: that I respect them as businesspeople, as the cultivators of one of the most rabid audiences outside of an actual cult that I'd ever seen or heard. That I am a fan first, and that I hope my appreciation of their work helps them understand why I cried.

Five minutes later? An email from the angrier of the two cohosts, saying this was the email they wanted to receive, the only enthusiasm they'd heard from the company so far. She says they want to move forward, to work together.

Ten minutes later? I take a hard look at my nonexistent savings account, my dignity, and email my boss. It's either me or the lawyer, I write. I feel the rush of testing how much the company needs me. How valuable, rather than unvaluable, I am.

Imagine you're sitting in a hotel room, having fired off an ultimatum, while unwrapping a third hamburger. You don't have the money to quit the job you just threatened to quit. But you've perhaps done the one thing women in the workplace aren't allowed to do: wield your anger. How would you feel? I feel triumphant. Then nauseous. Then I puke.

While sitting on the bathroom floor, I start receiving a series of phone calls and texts from everyone in the C-suite, saying how irreproachable the lawyer's behavior is. All words and no promise of action. But, words nonetheless, in response to my ultimatum.

With the nausea gone, the weight of my decision replaces it. Then comes fear. That is enough to get me to return to New York, to my desk, to continue the work. But not for long.

𝍸 𝍸 𝍸 |

Job 16

Catch the Errant Wave

> **A coward can't conquer anything because he can't conquer himself.**
>
> Herbert Kaufman, *Optimism—Its Market Value* (1909)

One of the first signs was the ink. It was everywhere. All over the white desktops of the small office we shared. On doorknobs throughout the coworking space. Occasionally, unknowingly smeared across my new business partner's screaming face, making him look like a rabid coal miner.

A sudden, all-encompassing, and charged obsession with expensive, leaky fountain pens had come over my new business partner, who I'll call Roger. It would be the first of many sudden, all-encompassing obsessions that I witnessed over the three years we worked together.

I admit I found it compelling at first. Here was someone who'd made it—with a drive to own it all, win it all. There was no gray with Roger—not in the way he approached his life or work. Just smeared black ink, everywhere.

Tryhards, so focused on the broader idea of success, tend to miss obvious signs.

When we met in 2018, Roger was an established name in radio and podcasting who had turned his obsession on me. He was starting his own podcast company, and I was going to build it for him.

He set a meeting, and I—lost in a creative black hole of my own making—took it.

* * *

I decided I wouldn't immediately agree to do the job if he offered it. The post-panic-attack, "it's him or me" Laura was going to be careful with her greatest asset: her work ethic. I wanted to thoroughly suss out the opportunity and the person at the center of it. Did the "millions" Roger said he had acquired for this venture actually exist? Did he—contrary to the rumors about him—truly want to start a company and stick with it?

I met Roger and his "honorary CFO"—a woman I'll call Marla—at a drab office space in Midtown. Marla and I would both watch as Roger made a show of receiving a physical check from the production company paying him his "millions." Then Marla would snatch the check away from Roger, for safekeeping.

Remembering it now, I never actually saw the check, just the check-shaped piece of paper he took and the big smile on his face. I also saw the faltering expression on "the honorary" CFO's face when Roger called her "the honorary CFO"—like she'd never heard this description associated with herself before.

From there, my suss-out meeting morphed into a full-on recruiting tour.

We speed-walked to a WeWork space to meet "the company's lawyer." It turned out that Roger had never met this lawyer in person before but had told the lawyer by email or phone about the millions of dollars ready to be invested in his podcast company.

The lawyer was slick, with expensive shoes and a British accent, and did not seem particularly agitated by Roger's assigning him an official position on the spot. Roger wrote a bunch of words and numbers on a dry-erase board—literally the phrase *millions of dollars*, Roger's ideal number of employees, *30* for the number of television shows the podcast company would sell each year, and the percentage of the company the lawyer would own (a rare arrangement) if he were to work with us. After exiting the WeWork, Roger said to me, "We should hire him, right?"

At that point there was no "we." I hadn't agreed to take the job. Roger was creating a series of performances to round up the "me" to "we." Our meeting was over, but Roger—always in motion—asked me to walk with him to his next appointment. "You know, we won't always agree," he said. "We will fight."

The "we" was everywhere. Like the arrangement was a done deal.

Now, as you read this, and as I write this from the perspective of time and more experience, you may be wondering why I didn't recognize all these red flags? Or, if I recognized them, why did I ignore them? When you're a striver who is always looking for the next, the best opportunity, the gleam of that opportunity can blind one's internal alert systems. Plus, at my previous jobs, I had spent so much time proving myself. Tirelessly. Over and over. And here was a person who said I was fully proven.

It had not occurred to me until I met Roger that I could be done with that phase of my work life. A week passed. Roger texted; he emailed; he Instagram direct messaged me. He called me in the middle of the day asking me to come visit office space for "our company."

It was a Brooklyn coworking space, much hipper than the drab Midtown affair we'd met in previously. Roger's assistant, who I'll call Scott, met me at the door. About my age, he projected a "professional assistant" busyness/weariness that involved dourly burying himself in his cell phone. And he carried a heaviness I immediately clocked.

Scott took me upstairs to Roger, who was yukking it up with the owner of the coworking space, talking about his millions of dollars, his television project with a famous writer and director, and agreeing that "we'd" shout out the name of the coworking space at the end of each podcast.

We received a tour of the space.

"We could turn that room," Roger said, gesturing to a glass conference room in the center of the floor, "into the recording studio."

"No, you can't," the owner of the coworking space said, pausing the tour. It was one of the few times I heard someone say no to Roger.

He rolled right through it.

We continued walking and talking.

Roger, turning his beam back on me, recounted the time he'd recorded one of figure skater Michelle Kwan's contemporaries, Sasha Cohen, for National Public Radio.

I must've gasped. I'd mentioned to Roger at our first meeting that I had a lifelong obsession with Michelle Kwan, forever considered the underdog of skating despite winning every single medal with the exception of Olympic gold.

Kwan and I were kindred spirits!

Roger trilled off details of his "huge" podcast deals, his connections to celebrities and political figures, and how these relationships would help the company. I ate it up. After the tour, in the lobby, Scott sunk into the couch beside me, while Roger excitedly pecked at his laptop.

"So, you're working here, right?" Roger said, looking up.

I said I needed time to decide. "Well, you have an email now." He held out his phone to show me the one he had just crafted, showing the peace of a fresh, empty Gmail inbox. A blank slate.

Constant texts, emails, and calls from Roger continued for the next week. Today, I'd consider this a badgering campaign. Then, I just saw green, an opportunity: Here was my chance to try out entrepreneurship without risking my own money. Entrepreneurship: something I said I'd never do after what I saw my father go through.

An employment contract was drafted, at the same salary I had at my job at the last podcast company, with the provision that if I didn't start by the following week I would no longer have the job. The first official lunch, where I met Roger, was two weeks before the contract came in.

Roger types aren't uncommon, particularly in the world of start-ups. I'm sure you've heard the phrase "fake it until you make it." That can be the mantra of start-ups, of inducing progress, sure. But beyond business, to their core, Rogers pray at the altar of that maxim. As a result, their insecurity stems from their urge to run far, far away from what they've admitted to themselves is at their core: the "fake it."

Now, imagine a Roger who has fallen into some kind of success. They succeeded in faking it until they've *kind of* made it. These Roger types often take a lot of bets and, as a result, one of them pans out: They created one company or product for something that suddenly had a consumer interest. That company may not have been well-run or functional (in fact, with Rogers, I can guarantee you they weren't well-run or functional), but the timing and optics were right. Once this happens, a Roger is suddenly a success. In an effort to further distance themselves from "faking it," Rogers adopt success as something inherent to them, full stop: a jewel to be protected at all costs.

Yet, the protection of that jewel turbocharges their Rogering.

Often, during this good run, they glom on to people with bold-faced names, to various degrees of stickiness. Suddenly, those notable people become key figures in their mythmaking, their ever-important self-managed optics. The known people, just by varying degrees of proximity, serve as a kind of reference point to their competence and relevance. And you, if dealing with this level of a Roger, will never, ever, hear the end of the name drops. You will hear the same stories about the same celebrities (regardless of your field) repeated to others as a way to impress. You will reflect on how these stories, when you first heard them, impressed you.

Here's the scariest part of a Roger to you, dear reader: If you're someone experiencing any level of self-doubt, or any desire to prove the work that you've already done, they'll be able to smell that insecurity on you. Because they know that scent. It's blood in the water, and a Roger is a shark who never stops moving. They know your desire for approval, and they will exploit that until you sign on the dotted line.

After I signed, Roger's obsession with me ended and the veil came down:

"The honorary CFO" was his personal accountant.

The "millions of dollars" were a projection based on a meeting he was sure would result in millions of dollars.

Roger had only thousands of investor dollars and quickly began integrating his personal funds into the podcast company to sustain basic operations.

Part of the urgency to sign me on was so that Roger could get another tranche of money for the one deal/show he had secured and needed me to produce.

Scott, his sad assistant, worked for a personal-assistant company and didn't actually assist Roger, exclusively. Mostly he would help me move large pieces of furniture around, assemble a WhisperRoom, and talk about his recent breakup—the center of the sadness he carried with him. Roger fired Scott due to a lack of funds, days after he told Scott he saw a full-time job at the company in his future.

Then paychecks stopped arriving.

Marla, "the honorary CFO," lent money to Roger to fill the gap. I was stuck, seeing the red lights coming toward me, unable to move out of the middle of the street.

The most dangerous, and impressive, aspect of a tryhard is the commitment. Once I make the decision to do something I will stick with it, until the bitter end.

The most dangerous aspect of a person driven by single-minded, short-lived obsession is what happens when the latest short-lived obsession burns out.

Roger's fountain pens, for example, were being thrown in the trash within the first month of his ink-fueled mania. But the ink remained on the desks. And, worse, an obsessive without a current obsession is a wrecking ball until he finds his next fixation. An unrelenting internal pressure builds up, without a specific target. It blows up randomly, catching fire to whatever is near. And I was the combustible fabric standing closest to Roger, during his fiery lulls.

"Stop talking to Marla," he snapped when I began asking questions about the finances of the company. "Marla charges by the hour."

We should've cratered. But this was a lucky time to be a professional in podcasting. Only a few truly experienced producers like myself and Roger existed on the national scene, and ventures suddenly needed us desperately.

Twelve weeks into my tenure, when I was beginning to doubt all my life decisions and planning to open a cat spa in a state without property taxes, executives from, what I'll call, the Big Entertainment Money company called us and set a meeting.

Roger's relative happened to be a top executive at Big Entertainment Money. I shrugged. Though nepotism made me itchy, I was allergic to failure.

That said, I thought it was a bit of a reach, our talking to a company in a totally different vertical, and told Roger so. We didn't need more distractions, I said, as we still hadn't made the one podcast Roger's initial investor had paid for.

Roger ignored me. The meeting that followed turned out to be the greatest stroke of financial luck I'll ever see in my lifetime.

At the meeting Roger did his thing: He pointed to his personal résumé, his as-yet-to-be-realized television show with the famous writer-director, and his past success in public radio. I said pretty much nothing: The suits were in the room to talk to their boss's relative.

A week after the initial meeting with the Big Entertainment Money company, Roger's relative called and said his company was interested in creating a joint venture—a co-owned podcast production company.

I got to work making business plans and spreadsheets. Roger adjusted his story, telling anyone who would listen about the "millions" of dollars he would soon be getting from Big Entertainment Money.

Every ounce of my attention became focused on making this joint venture actually happen.

When the deal closed, an article came out in a Hollywood trade about the joint venture, which I co-owned, and someone tweeted "I guess Laura Mayer's cats will be treated like Karl Lagerfeld's cats now." I didn't blink.

We now had an operating budget in the millions.

Roger's proclamations had finally come true.

I made myself the chief operating officer and received a salary that was more than double what I was originally being paid. We hired more than a dozen people to work with us. We multiplied all our production goals by ten.

Roger, keen to live in the "as soon as possible," as much as possible, thrived on the urgency. He called every famous person he even vaguely knew and tried to get them involved with our venture, which would continue to make "millions," he said. When Roger invited Danny and me to his apartment for a celebratory dinner, he greeted Danny by saying "Welcome to the one percent." We were not part of the 1 percent, and can you even imagine someone saying that phrase to you with a straight face?

So Roger had faked it until he made it, and I was along for the ride. Is this how people became successful? I don't lie to anyone but myself, and at this time, I accepted our stroke of luck and even felt like a damn genius for about a month. Here I was, at the top of the podcast mountain, and maybe I finally deserved it?

With more access to actual money, Roger's ambitious obsessions grew. He roped the famous writer-director he claimed to be working with into the joint venture, committing much of our budget to a nested joint venture within our joint venture. A matryoshka doll of EBITA (earnings before interest, taxes, and amortization—an acronym that measures a company's profitability and an acronym that makes it sound like I went to business school, which I have not). One day I walked into the office at 9:00 a.m. to Roger screaming, red-faced, into the phone to someone in LA that they needed to join a project "or else." It was 6:00 a.m. in LA. That didn't go over well. His real-deal television producer friend called him and said to "not get ahead of his skis."

Roger, as far as I know, never looked at the budget or attended a finance meeting. He bragged to our bosses at Big Entertainment Money that he didn't understand the mechanisms of how podcasts made money. The Big Entertainment Money company's execs smiled and chuckled. I turned into a viscous liquid.

But what fun in those early days! There were first-class tickets from New York to LA. There were meetings with celebrities. I sat in the Delta Sky Club for the first time in my life, where an expensively dressed drunk woman, eavesdropping on a conversation I was having on the phone with a producer said, "Good job firing him." I hadn't fired anyone. I think she admired my semi-expensive jacket and assumed I was firing someone to pay for that piece of outerwear.

There was, memorably, a Big Entertainment Money retreat in Miami at which I met Harry Styles, shook his hand, and stammered "Podcasts are cool" before skittering away from the conversation as quickly as possible. His charm was like staring into the sun. Later that night he led a toast to the attendees, which ended with "to Big Entertainment Money, the greatest Big Entertainment Money company in the world!" I poured my tequila shot in the empty glass of the SVP sitting next to me, who'd spent the evening telling me why his wife shouldn't be mad that he rarely saw his children.

So there was glamour, and there was money. Cool. What there wasn't? Podcasts being made. Why?

"Everyone's ideas are bad," Roger would say, like a prayer, every day, multiple times a day. All the producers "didn't know how to make radio"—never mind we were actually making podcasts.

I began running regular podcast development meetings with the producers. Standard operating procedure—I'd done this at every one of my previous podcast jobs. We were meant to develop both true-crime series and business interview shows—ideally shows that intersected both genres. For the true-crime series, I set out the basic framework that the shows should have a crime (a business scam, generally), a central character who ran the scam, and either a conclusion or an ongoing legal battle that could be followed. For the business shows, I said we needed to focus on formats that allowed Roger to interview people who were in the process of creating unusual but successful companies.

On one early morning, Roger found out I was helping our producers develop show ideas (otherwise known as doing their jobs), and he turned apoplectic.

"Everyone's ideas are bad!" he messaged me—his ideas excluded, of course.

Feeling like I'd overstepped, he began firing off cruel

messages to producers and to me on Slack. The gist of these messages were, "None of you know what you're doing."

Managerial tip: If you ever want to drastically demotivate a team, make it clear to the team members that you believe they don't have any of the skills to be successful in the jobs they were hired to do. We were supposed to be taking all ideas directly from Roger, apparently, despite his consistent absences, many having to do with the next goal he was trying to achieve (creating and showrunning a television show). The pursuit of this dream involved going to LA a lot and screaming at agents and television producers at 9:00 a.m. EST a.k.a. 6:00 a.m. PST. Rolling those calls took a lot of time and effort!

When I walked into his ink-stained office to address these messages, he yelled, "Why don't you go ask your husband whether he thinks you behaved reasonably."

Why. Don't. You. Go. Ask. Your. Husband. Whether. He. Thinks. You. Behaved. Reasonably.

(I did ask Danny. "Fuck that guy." Bless Danny.)

The casual sexism turned direct and went beyond me. Everyone who was "bad" to work with had been, in his estimation, a woman. Anyone who he knew to be "good" was a man. There was "bad," and there was "good," and there was no in-between.

I'm not letting myself off the hook here. These signs, specifically around sexism, were there from the beginning of our time working together, basically as soon as his obsession with hiring me was sated. I was "like" another female executive he knew, but "good," he told me once, which is why he'd wanted to hire me.

Sorry, ladies. I now fully know those statements were never a compliment to me. They were about his ego and his low estimations of all of us. And I, insecure, accepted any praise as a sign of a goodness I didn't yet believe I had.

When my blood pressure dropped, I launched into triage mode. Surely these comments would stop with me. And I could take them, I thought. I could be called unreasonable, go home and "talk to my husband" about my behavior, and get a full-throated and protective "Fuck that guy." I could be the dam onto which the bile cascaded and stop it from rolling down further. I'd end the cruel Slacking. I was managing everyone, and this was part of management.

Looking back, that was, at best, wishful thinking and, more accurately, a deeply hurtful miscalculation to the team.

The joint venture wasn't going well. Increasingly, the Big Entertainment Money company called me to complain.

"The spreadsheet guys," Roger called them dismissively, when I reported the calls.

The spreadsheet guys were the ones who watched our cash flow, who saw the ballooning budgets that could trigger an immediate shutdown of our joint venture.

Roger's wild spending did not slow. Trips around the

country for unconfirmed interviews, unneeded astronomical salaries to court talent, first-class flights to LA for meetings that never were on the books to begin with.

His rages persisted, too. At the same dinner where Harry Styles led a tequila toast to the best Big Entertainment Money company in the world, Roger took a business call that enraged him so much he knocked over a table. He was several drinks in and caught wind that a reporter he was trying to "crush" (by that he meant "hire") wasn't playing ball with deal terms he was trying to offer her. Did I know the deal terms? Of course not. These were between Roger and his agents. There was literal foam coming out of his mouth as he stalked away.

"That's Roger!" the SVP who didn't see his children said.

This was not the right room for me to be in.

So I returned to the comfort of my hotel room, the nicest room I'd ever slept in. A room I'd been escorted to by a man in a suit who I think expected a tip, but I was too gobsmacked by the pomp to think of that. This room had an actual couch in it. I've stayed in motel rooms without toilets. This one had a toilet *and* a bathtub, shower, kitchenette, plus a large refrigerator. It would've been the nicest domicile I'd ever create in *The Sims*, let alone actually inhabit. I didn't even do my customary check for bedbugs on the baseboard of the bed.

I was being paid more money than I thought I deserved, invited into spaces that I suspect others were surprised

I was in, dealing with the most malignantly chaotic person I'd ever encountered, and trying to dodge and weave around him to avoid a nightmare with the large staff I was running. The situation was impossible.

"If anyone can manage it, you can," Danny would say, pointing to the situations I handled as a kid with my family.

But significant parts of me were awakening to the fact that I didn't want to repeat that same cycle. Which, let me tell you, was, and continues to be, inconvenient!

At the time, I wasn't yet willing to give it up—this success I felt like I deserved, my burnished ego, how good things looked on paper, my Karl Lagerfeld cats, one of whom was able to get thyroid treatment at a radioactive iodine clinic on the Upper West Side where they referred to her food and toys as her "luggage." Wasn't this what I'd worked for—every day of my life? So I propped myself up with naps, Nintendo, sending more emails than any one person should send, and burying my head into the sand of the compound interest I knew my newly flush retirement account would soon benefit from.

卌 卌 卌 ||

Job 17

Don't Go to Couple's Therapy with Your Business Partner

> **The trouble was, I hated the idea of serving men in any way. I wanted to dictate my own thrilling letters.**
>
> Sylvia Plath, *The Bell Jar*

Four events happened in quick succession: Sober Roger insisted we go to couple's therapy; drunk Roger unleashed the curious ire of a late-night television host; COVID-19 hit; and I got very complicatedly pregnant.

First, the couple's therapist.

Apparently my husband, Danny, wasn't doing the trick in terms of keeping me reasonable. So Roger proposed a solution: a visit to the couple's therapist he'd seen with his last business partner, a detail from his past I'd never heard before. The therapist was a perfectly nice, older woman in Columbus Circle who didn't take insurance. We met with her after the first true impasse of our business partnership: meaning, I didn't buckle to Roger's rage, and he was mad about it. Roger made it clear to the therapist that, like last time, he would be paying (our company paid for the sessions).

"Do you see a road to fix this partnership?" the therapist asked me.

"Yes, if I am treated as what I am, which is the co-founder of this company," I said.

In therapy and in life Roger had two modes: righteous indignation and deep, unnecessarily over-the-top atonement.

In atonement he was the *worst*. He was an *idiot*. He was *scum*! The flagellating series would build accordingly.

The therapist seemed pleased. She gave us worksheets, which we never referenced again. She and Roger communicated between sessions. She never called me. We saw her three or four times before Roger, once again, blew out of town. As someone who has been in approximately one thousand sessions of personal therapy, I believe in it. I believe in the capacity to change. What this was wasn't therapy. It was an attempt by Roger to hire a professional to get me to act "reasonably." To be fair to Roger, like any other hardheaded person, I am capable of unreasonableness. In this case, however, I was actually trying to make reason out of complete chaos. He didn't want to see that.

* * *

It was his blowout trip to Los Angeles that raised the ire of a late-night television host.

In February 2020 Roger decided to pursue a lead related to Jeffrey Epstein's sex-trafficking ring. The lead came from a chef with a reputation that Roger found intriguing and who lived in Los Angeles.

Roger had been gone a few days when I received a late-night text from a friend who worked at Roger's famous friend's production company. My friend wondered if I'd heard about this dinner thing with Roger.

"No. What dinner thing?"

Over the days that followed, I would piece together the story. It took several tries and went something like this: A well-known victim of Jeffrey Epstein, Roger, and an ex–television reporter walked into a restaurant in Los Angeles. Why this restaurant? According to hearsay and some light research, the restaurant is owned by someone who is dubiously connected to Jeffrey Epstein and this well-known victim. The victim, Roger, and the ex–television reporter planned to spend a ton of money at the restaurant, then they'd say they wanted to pay compliments to the chef. Then they hoped the chef would come by their table. He'd then be confronted by the highly traumatized victim of Jeffrey Epstein. The victim would then record herself accusing the chef of his relationship with Epstein and explain the chef's impact on her life. This would, somehow, figure into a podcast.

Several thousands of dollars and lots of wine later, compliments went to the chef, but he did not emerge. He wasn't at the restaurant. The victim cried; Roger recorded it. Unsatisfied, not wanting the night to go to waste, Roger found out about a political fundraiser happening in one of the restaurant's private dining rooms.

He and the ex–television reporter used the famous writer-director's name to gain entrée to the private dining room. There they approached an ex-*SNL* star and ex-politician (the same person) and said to him, "Do you know you are dining at the restaurant of a convicted sex trafficker?" Never mind there was no conviction or proof of this claim, the ex-politician responded with something like "No, I did not." Larry David and Patton Oswalt were also in the room. Roger and the reporter were kicked out of the restaurant.

That wasn't the end of it.

Once Roger returned to where he was staying (in someone's guesthouse), he sent an email to the customer service team at Resy, the app where he'd made the night's restaurant reservation, furious that the chef he'd meant to snag would not come out to atone for his (unproven, dubious) sins.

Then, by all accounts, Roger passed out.

Turns out Resy customer service did not pass out. The claim was forwarded to the chef's lawyer. The chef's lawyer then got one of his best friends and supporters involved, a famous late-night television show host. That late-night television host reached Roger's famous director friend and asked if he knew that Roger had used his famous name to gain access to a private fundraiser, where he and a reporter had drunkenly confronted a politician about his false proximity to a scandal involving Jeffrey Epstein.

No, the famous friend did not know that.

Roger was in full-scale *I am slime* mode, and likely fairly hungover, when he called me in Brooklyn.

"Something happened."

He explained the entire thing.

I said, "This sounds very bad."

He said, "I'm going to stop drinking," and then called himself "terrible" upwards of a dozen times. He had the same phone call with the Big Entertainment Money company, with his famous director friend, perhaps with a nearby Starbucks barista. Concerned about my association with all of this, I called my lawyer. I told none of the producers at the company what was going on.

A few weeks later, COVID hit. We all vacated the coworking space (fun fact: a common autocorrect for *coworking space* is *cowering space*, which has generally been my experience). The ink was still smeared all over Roger's office.

One of the "spreadsheet guys," during a finance meeting, lamented to me: "I wish we had put a force majeure clause in your joint venture contract," referring to wishing he could shut down the joint venture due to the pandemic. "Never going to make that mistake again!"

Reassuring! Again, I didn't tell my producers.

Roger escaped the city with his family early on and moved into an Airbnb estate. He stayed for a month, then two, then three, then he began making capital improvements to the property on behalf of its absent Nordic owners.

During this time, Roger was soothed. The combination of a global health crisis and the details of installing wiring in a stranger's home calmed him. Zoom was the touchpoint for the entire production team, for the entire world at that point. When he showed up to meetings, having that distance from Roger gave me—and I suspect everyone at the production company that worked with him—a lot of relief. No one missed the physical proximity to his chaos.

Still, the producers feared layoffs. I worried about Big Entertainment Money shutting us down. But with Roger distracted, we finally began making and releasing podcasts. One weekend he manically created a pilot for a daily podcast about COVID's economic impact, which he insisted he would host and produce himself. It was unstructured, rambling, full of the kind of mania I'd grown used to. I listened to it, and I told him that it didn't work, especially as he was meant to be the CEO of the company, which meant he should be managing the overall strategy of the company and serving as its day-to-day leader, especially to the Big Entertainment Money company. I also said producers had full dance cards, which meant everyone had at least two podcasts in production or development. With the blessed distance of COVID, he responded to my feedback over email with "Fine." He later bragged to employees about his ability to graciously take "critical feedback."

The producers and I continued making podcasts, and Roger put himself more or less out of the picture, with the exception of suddenly coming up with get-rich-quick schemes involving foreign companies investing "billions" in podcasts or creating "apps." I pressed him for details on the apps he wanted to create. He had no more detail than that, just "apps." He was grasping for another cultural hook to grab on to, to leave podcasting behind and make his "billions" elsewhere. After the ill-fated Resy incident, Big Entertainment Money's suits were keeping a closer eye on Roger's behavior. Someone from the mothership had been brought in to help mitigate his damage. That gave me further cover from Roger and someone to make meaningful eye contact with over Zoom, my eyes pleading for confirmation that whatever happened to be coming out of Roger's mouth this time didn't make sense, right? Right?

* * *

In the summer of 2020 I did the thing I do every four or so years: I decided I should probably go to business school. I bought GMAT books and signed up for a Zoom prep class on the weekends. I sat at my giant wooden table and worked through the workbook during the week and attended the Zoom prep class for about four weekends before I realized I did not, in fact, want to go to business school. I didn't tell Danny I'd quit. Instead, I dutifully retired to my office on Saturday mornings for class and proceeded to build decadent Sims neighborhoods, replete with gossip since I'd made every Sim look identical and given them the same name: Laura Mayer.

It was at that point that I realized it was time to have a baby. I was thirty-three and financially stable for the first time in my life. I was, due to my diligent weight training over the previous five years, as healthy as I ever was going to be. Lulu the cat had finished her radioactive iodine thyroid treatment, so all of her radioactive shit had been disposed of.

I fell almost immediately pregnant. Danny began an MFA program in September 2020. He left for his first day of night school, and I took a pregnancy test. I FaceTimed Danny after class at Fort Greene Park. He cheered, with two face masks taped to his face, while hoisting his kick scooter in the air.

I went to the ob-gyn to have my HCG levels tested and to have an ultrasound. My HCG levels were very high, and there appeared to be two sacs forming.

"This is, very likely, a multiple pregnancy."

The twin having twins.

On election night the bleeding began, and it continued into the night. We went to the ob-gyn the next day. It was so early in the pregnancy that I was anticipating a miscarriage. They found one heartbeat that day—Joanna's heartbeat—and what appeared to be a subchorionic hematoma, a probably benign annoyance they told us, which could cause bleeding for an indeterminate amount of time. I was put on bed rest.

I told Roger about the pregnancy situation. He "truly understood." Another hallmark of Roger, his use of the word *truly*. Few things weren't truly something—truly good, truly bad, truly moving, truly horrible.

The bleeding continued. I was kept on rest. I found the heat of my laptop helped with the cramping. In December Danny bought a Littmann stethoscope, the type of purchase only first-time parents would make, to see if we could hear the baby between OB appointments. We definitely heard my heart.

Around this time Roger started acting up again. Setting up meetings with companies, promising them the world, and reporting back that millions of dollars were right around the corner. Speaking of millions, the podcast he'd made as part of Resy-gate had cost one million dollars. A similarly research-heavy narrative show without the extraneous spending would've cost a (still substantial) $400,000. This pushed Roger further into a money-hungry tailspin to try to save face.

Right before the New Year in 2021, Roger sent me an email. He wanted to fire everyone in the company and pivot to making that app he'd been talking about. An app to do what? That part still wasn't clear. This was his "last chance" at making his fortune, he said. If I wasn't interested in this direction, he said, he would walk.

I wrote back that it sounded like he should walk.

And that's when Roger declared war on me and, incidentally, my unborn child.

He called the Big Boss and said I was pushing him out of the company. He called all the "suits" and "spreadsheet guys" to say the same thing. Otherwise, he disappeared from all company communication.

I called my lawyer. I hadn't told anyone at the company what was going on.

I got a call from Big Entertainment Money, asking if Roger had "done anything" to me.

"Define *done* and *anything*," I said.

The conversation moved on, but I understood what Big Entertainment Money was looking for: an easy out for a clear violation. The trouble with the situation with Roger is he had "done" nothing legally actionable but was, on a daily basis to any person of a perceived lower status than him, reprehensible and impossible to work with.

The Big Entertainment Money company designed a Bake-Off. They'd hear my business plan—to slim down the company, lower costs, but to continue making quality podcasts—and Roger's business plan—to fire everyone and invest ten million dollars in building an app—and decide who would stay.

I was four months pregnant, still bleeding, and doing all-nighters revising the budget and our business plan, which was work I couldn't do inside of the scope of my day-to-day job. I presented my plan, over Zoom, to a combination of the "suits" and the "spreadsheet guys." I called my lawyer. And I waited.

All the conversations from there, about my fate within the company, went through lawyers. They went with my business plan, so long as a round of layoffs happened immediately.

Lawyers lawyered, and I stayed. Roger's lawyer reached out to my lawyer to attempt to mend fences, to mount a fight against Big Entertainment Money to buy out the joint venture. I passed on that opportunity.

Roger was gone. The last time Roger reached out to me directly was on January 6, 2021. Memorable! I later heard he was paid to leave, which was typical but vexing. The first round of layoffs happened. The bleeding stopped. I was given a highfalutin corporate title for accounting purposes but continued running the programming, keeping the budget, and managing the staff as I had been throughout the entire venture. It finally looked like I was running a company, even though that company no longer existed.

I worked out my maternity leave plan with the suits. And, to be clear, this was my idea: I'd be completely off of work for three weeks, then I'd return to work for four weeks, then I'd take half days as needed. "No need to backfill me," I said. "I mean, look at the budget!"

Then, one afternoon that spring, I was creating a proposal for a branded podcast and I had a seizure at my home desk. After I came to, I ran to Danny in the living room, ripped off my shirt because I was so hot, laid on my left side on the bathroom floor, and told him to take my blood pressure. Some astounding number came up: two hundred over *get me to the hospital.* I remember thinking, very clearly, as I waited on the bathroom floor for the ambulance to arrive that if I died it would be okay. The baby, who we'd started calling Jojo, just needed to make it.

The paramedics arrived, took my blood pressure, and put me in the ambulance. I had a bucket to puke in and great eavesdropping material, as two of the medics had recently partied together in New Jersey.

"What happens in Jersey, stays in Jersey," I shouted into the puke bucket.

In the hospital I learned that the attending nurse loved EDM music, his mother, and that he didn't have the bedside manner not to gasp and throw his hand over his mouth when I told him I was only thirty-two weeks pregnant.

I was hooked up to all kinds of machines—tracking my blood pressure, my heart rate, the baby's heart rate, and the contractions I was having. I gave blood. I peed in cups. I Slacked my deputy that I was in the hospital and wouldn't be in any meetings for the rest of the day.

"You have preeclampsia," the doctor said.

What did that mean? Medically, it means the placenta didn't develop properly, due to the blood vessels that are meant to supply it. At an emergency OB appointment the next day I found out it also meant, because I wasn't due for two months, they could deliver the baby then and risk her life. Or put me on blood pressure medication, have me visit a high-risk OB twice a week, stay on bed rest, and risk my life. I chose the latter.

"I can still work, right?" I remember asking the OB.

"Uh, well . . ." she hesitated.

"What about ten percent?"

"I'll write you a note," she said.

The note read that Ms. Mayer was to refrain from any stressful work for the duration of her pregnancy. I rounded that up and emailed the Big Entertainment Money company explaining the situation and said I could work 10 percent of the time in my current state.

To everyone at the Big Entertainment Money's credit, they said a resounding "no" to my proposal. I was put on short-term disability immediately. I took to bed with my cat Hector, on what I would later call our babymoon. I wasn't working my current job, but I had a new one: to stay as alive and calm as possible. And I took this job seriously.

Danny set up the baby monitor early to watch me from his perch in the living room. I peed in a bucket next to my bed. We packed the hospital bag. We bought preemie clothes. Nearly every time we went to the high-risk OB my blood pressure was high, Jojo's heart rate was elevated. The doctor would say something like "If things don't stabilize, then you'll need to go to the hospital." Every time, within five minutes, we stabilized. I respect authority on a biological level and, at that time, it seemed to extend to fetus Jojo.

I made it to thirty-eight weeks before they induced labor. In the delivery room the nurse asked me what my labor plan was so she could write it on a whiteboard. I told her: "For the baby to be alive and for me to be alive." Simple enough. I thanked the doctors between each push for four hours.

When she was born, she didn't immediately cry. Danny and I, though, immediately started screaming, "Is she alive?" "Is she fucking alive?!" Absolutely losing it, as they worked on her in the Panda Warmer.

My doula, who I met in person only for the delivery, tried to distract me by pointing at "how beautiful" the placenta was.

I turned to her and said, "I don't wanna see that thing. It tried to fucking kill us!"

Jojo, a.k.a. Joanna, was born healthy at seven pounds, seven ounces, weighing in at three times my birth weight (I was a preemie). She had long fingers and even longer fingernails.

After the flurry of activity in the Panda Warmer ended, one of the doctors thought to ask, "When was she born?"

"Let's call it six fifteen a.m."

She'll never have an accurate astrological chart, and she'll resent me for this as a teen.

Preeclampsia generally resolves when the placenta exits. After holding Joanna, both of us crying, and after I slammed some cow's milk, they took the epidural out, put Joanna back in my arms, put us in a wheelchair, and wrapped a sheet around the chair and me so we wouldn't fall out of it. I could tell, then, that I wasn't in the best shape. Though, having never delivered a baby before, I didn't have anything to compare it to. When I was holding Joanna while being wheeled to our shared recovery room, I was lucid enough to hear and remember the nurses congratulating me.

We were left to our own devices in the recovery room. The head nurse kept calling Danny "Dad" dryly, and finally grew tired of bringing us pitchers of water and gave him the code to the water room. Danny tried to take photos of Joanna's first bath, through the windows of the nursery, and he got shooed away. We stayed in the recovery room for two days and one night, then we were discharged.

I walked to her first pediatrician's appointment the next day. A few days after that, Joanna's Nonna watched Joanna while Danny and I went to the grocery store alone. This was the first time I'd been somewhere without Jo since I knew she was in there in the first place. That song where Dido and Eminem duet, "Stan," came on the speakers at the supermarket. I began crying at the existence of the year 2000 and thought to myself, *I don't feel right.* I pushed it to the side. Joanna was healthy; this was just sleep deprivation and hormones.

One evening I was sitting in our living room with Danny, Danny's mother, and Joanna, when I started feeling that old tight, hot, *I'm going to lose consciousness while writing a branded podcast proposal* feeling. I went to the bedroom, and

Danny took my blood pressure: 190 over *not again*! I went to the ER. The best they could do for me was give me some blood pressure medication and refer me back to my OB. I went to my OB, and the best she could do was give me some blood pressure medication.

I kept saying, "I don't feel right."

She kept saying, "You just had a baby."

I was back in bed, taking my blood pressure every two hours, and trying to help care for my new child as much as I possibly could. Nonna went back home. Danny did the night shifts, and I did the mornings and early afternoons, like the second and third stews on *Below Deck*.

One morning I was feeding Joanna and thinking, *I really don't feel right.*

Danny woke up for his shift, and I went up to the roof of the building and did a Headspace meditation, "Navigating Difficult Times." At 8:00 p.m. I went to the bedroom and turned on the white noise machine to an unheard-of decibel. Danny came in, took my temperature, and discovered that I had a 104-degree fever. We called the OB practice, and they sent me back to the hospital where I gave birth.

Unlike the first time I went to the ER, I was just postpartum enough (yet not at the magical six-week mark when OBs can discharge you from their care) not to be seen in the maternity ward. Instead, I was admitted to the place for vaginas in trouble, I guess: Mount Sinai's sex crimes triage unit.

I sat alone in a room overhearing the horrifying accounts

of a series of women who had been sexually assaulted that summer night. The attending doctor was charismatic and coiffed in a way that made me wonder if he had a popular TikTok account, but he wasn't super up to the task of whatever was going on with me.

He took a sample from my, ahem, birth canal, and said, "Wow, that doesn't look right." He left the room.

I was then seen by a very young OB/GYN who was accompanied by a female security guard.

"I can't be in the room with you alone," he said.

He then had me insert the ultrasound wand myself. I was sent back to the sex crimes amphitheater.

I'd been in the hospital for about six hours by that point. They did a chest X-ray. A CT scan of my abdomen. Another gynecological exam. And then they forgot about me. I sat on the bed, listening to police officers discuss the sex crimes that were being investigated, attempting to pump milk for Joanna, and wondering what the hell was going on. I called Danny, crying, saying they'd forgotten about me. I wheeled myself, my IV bag slung over my neck like a mink to the main area of the ER and asked if someone could please let me know what they were going to do with me. Someone promised they would let me know. I wheeled myself back to my bed.

An hour passed.

The young OB/GYN came in and said, excitedly, "Did you see what I found?" in the tone of a kid who discovered a really cool stick in the yard.

I said, "No."

He said, "Possible remnants of birth!" He left before I could ask what that meant.

I called Danny, again, crying. Danny called the ER switchboard and somehow got to the most powerful woman in the entire ward: the receptionist who had been working there forever; she was, potentially, immortal.

She was not, however, a medical doctor. She came into the room and said, "It's funny. I was just talking to my boyfriend about postpartum . . . what is it?"

"Depression?" I cried.

"That's it! And here you are."

Minutes later, a fleet of doctors came in to see me at last. The immortal receptionist had sounded the alarm. They discharged me with the strongest antibiotic you can take outside of a hospital, along with orders to follow up with my GP. My six weeks under the care of my OB/GYN were over.

It turned out my liver enzymes were through the roof. So was my blood pressure. I was put on different medications that I had to take at different times of day. Danny printed out a paper chart to mark what medications I had taken at what time and taped it to our bedroom wall. I was so weak that I couldn't hold the baby while I was standing up. I do remember holding my head between my knees to try to lower my blood pressure, watching Danny as he cradled Joanna—the size of a giant football at that point—while marking off the time that I took the blood pressure medication on the paper chart.

Finally, six months after Joanna was born, I saw a hepatologist (a doctor who specializes in livers). My blood tests and vital signs were returning to normal. She sat and looked through my past tests, then, calmly, told me that I had preeclampsia and HELLP syndrome.

HELLP syndrome is pretty much what it sounds like: bad. It's in the preeclampsia family in the way that rattlesnakes are in the same category as boa constrictors. HELLP syndrome leads to death in up to 25 percent of cases, through strokes or liver ruptures. Like preeclampsia and a lot of diseases of pregnancy, it's not well understood. The doctors didn't know what to do with me in part because they didn't know to look for, or what to do with HELLP.

But, yeah, I guess it makes sense why I wasn't feeling so great. I was on maternity leave from the Big Entertainment Money company. My new jobs, now that the baby was alive, were to figure out how to get healthy and to keep keeping the baby alive. I took my full maternity leave, joining just one meeting during my time away.

While I was on leave a new head of podcasts was hired at the Big Entertainment Money company. I heard this secondhand. Suddenly, people who reported to me were being invited to his meetings. The company was moving on. It was clear that my executive presence was no longer required. But with a new baby and new health problems, I was once again in a bind: I needed health insurance, and I wasn't sure if I was going to be able to get another job in the condition I was then in. I called my lawyer.

She extracted me from the company. I left with nearly a year of paid health insurance and some of my salary.

The entire fancy fiasco was financially incredibly positive for me. I was paid twice as much as I'd ever made at a job before. I saved two-thirds of that money. I paid off my student loans. My retirement account floweth over. But at what cost?

There was also my growing—let's call it like it is—jealousy over nearly a dozen of my friends or past colleagues getting rich, rich, rich during the podcast boom. We're talking house-buying money plus-a-boat money plus-never-having-to-work-again money. But in my case, I'd never gotten paid for not working, ever. It felt luxurious—in a delusional way.

And I didn't quite know what to do with myself. I felt like I failed at being a big shot. I was now, through Joanna's existence, more than just my job, but not on the terms I'd imagined.

I'd harbored a secret plan to become less ambitious once the baby was born, but I had to put my work failure into context first, for myself and the listening public.

So I did what everyone in America was doing at that time . . .

Job 18

Record Thyself, Publish It on the Internet

Jumping is the only way how to stand on the air.

Joanna Blondell (my child)

If you're an adult standing next to a stroller, gazing at a house you covet, passersby tend to give you the benefit of the doubt and do not assume you're actively snooping. I used this to my advantage a lot in the spring of 2022.

Joanna and I stood in front of various coveted homes on a regular basis in her first year of life.

Sometimes I'd put on my sunglasses to examine molding, bay windows, new versus original woodwork. Sometimes I'd focus on a topiary. Joanna, in her early months, would sleep on these walks. An ideal snooping companion. As she came into consciousness, she became a pointer, an alarming gesture coming from anyone other than a baby. This habit made us a bit more of a spectacle for my purposes but still unassuming.

By this time, I was regularly bringing recording equipment along. Danny often joined. Once I forced Danny to pause and stand with the stroller, me, and my microphone in front of the Gray House.

"Describe the house," I instructed, the microphone ball in Danny's face.

Danny was no stranger to my fixation on the Gray House.

"It's a gray house," he said tentatively. He was not a willing participant in my new scheme. Still, he went into a short history of Victorian Flatbush. Until I cut him off.

"So the owner of the house," I said, forcing a shift in subtopics.

Danny tensed. "Oh, I already hate this."

Danny was referring to the podcast I was making. On my own. With no financial backing. And, more specifically, the legal risk I was opening myself up to in discussing a private residence on a public podcast. I had tentatively named it *Shameless Acquisition Target*. A reference to the Gray House I coveted and, really, so much else. The Gray House was my postpartum lodestar.

Still recording, I told Danny all the publicly available information I'd discovered about the house and its owner.

"Her father is a famous litigator," I concluded, after a thirty-second information dump.

"Okay, I am already bothered by this. A litigator! You better bleep this out so hard," Danny insisted.

In the first episode of the podcast I did bleep it out—well, most of it. I respect privacy. But I was not going to mince words about my aims:

"Despite Danny's . . . discomfort . . . I'm going to use this moment as an opportunity to, ahem, set an intention and start to put some *Shameless*ness back into my life: I am going to figure out a way, somehow, someday, to live in this goddamn house. And this is how you can help me do that . . ."

* * *

On its face, the show was a podcast about, well, the podcast industry. It ran for six episodes. The gimmick: I was publicly declaring, proclaiming, bullhorning (to the professional podcasting industry and anyone else who was listening) that I wanted a piece of the podcast windfall that all the audio talent around me had managed to pull down during the past five years. I wanted to get mine! And, I accepted PayPal, Venmo, cash, or the Gray House as payment.

I was willing to sell every bit of the podcast and many bits of myself—*Shameless*ly—to get it. For sale? The RSS feed, all advertising space, merchandise, the movie rights, my life rights, any IP that I could possibly squeeze from the show, and whatever else wasn't nailed down.

The absurdity of the proposition was a way to demonstrate the distance podcasting had moved away from its "roots." What were we doing making podcasts just for the purpose of becoming TV shows? We were supposed to be true believers, people who had chosen to work in podcasting and radio. We were supposed to be making actually good audio series, for the series' sake.

The show also made clear that I was in it for the money, honey, and that I knew how to make a hit.

And if anyone wanted to call me with a full-time job offer, I'd accept that, too.

Instead of hiding behind a boss or a business partner or a company name, I put myself front and center. To wit:

I interviewed my dad about his business failures, on Father's Day. It was the first conversation we'd ever had about my family's money trouble.

I was the first person to tell the story of how the 2015–2022 podcast bubble was about to pop. I did this by putting names to the various companies and people involved with the sector's overvaluation. The podcast and radio community is so small that people whispered bits and pieces of this story in bars. I shouted it in public.

I publicly baited podcasts, hosts, and public radio shows to feature my show. In fact, I did a lot of public baiting. In each episode I sold an ad. I featured the company who bought the ad in my show and revealed exactly how much they coughed up. The financials of podcasting, to be clear, are not something that was then discussed in podcasts. So that approach felt risqué. To take it a step further, at the end of the ad I'd often address the current company's direct competitors (some of whom I named) to outbid their competition for an ad on the next episode of the show.

At the end of each episode, I detailed exactly how much of my own money I was spending on the podcast (a fair bit!) and how much I was making (not much!).

I wanted the show to be fun. I made music. I hired many voice actors from the creative work-for-hire website Fiverr. These voice actors recurred as characters throughout the series. The final episode was a musical that I wrote and produced in fourteen days, with absolutely no musical background (I'll let you be the judge on how that turned out). I documented my growing unemployment insecurity, most notably in an episode titled "Money Hunger Worry Fest," that I wrote while stomping around Brooklyn in green Crocs fretting about my cash flow. I burned some industry bridges along the way. I let the listeners know just enough about my backstory. In one episode I said, "I saw how [my father's] business failings caused me to not have a full pair of gloves for several Chicago winters. How I hid my hands from my teachers so they wouldn't know." I was the everygirl who'd had enough "and was not gonna take it anymore!"

Every investment opportunity generated by the podcast—and bungled by me—was recorded for listeners' pleasure. At one point, I recorded myself in a Hollywood pitch meeting in which I explained the half-baked television version of the *Shameless Acquisition Target* podcast as a mix of "*Parasite* meets *Fleabag* meets *House Hunters International*."

Later, recorded for posterity, I went directly to my lifelong idol, *This American Life*'s creator, Ira Glass, and asked him to buy my podcast "for a dollar" or to hire me.

"I will buy your podcast for one dollar, but it ends there" was his response.

A good response! But one that, ultimately, left me with a type of tender embarrassment that only comes from a hurt rooted in childhood.

As I said to my therapist at the time, "It's less 'Don't meet your idols' and more 'Don't show up to the figurative house of your childhood idol just to invite him to symbolically shoot you down.'"

Ultimately, I sold the RSS feed of the show and a fair bit of advertising space. I recouped the costs for making the show. I broke even. I also, through someone hearing the show, was somehow offered a full-time job at a storied news organization.

I was not able to buy the Gray House or even a gray house with these proceeds. But I'd returned to my LobStar of the Week roots. I put myself entirely out there, to practically everyone I've ever known and worked with, in front of the object of success that eludes me: stability via home ownership. It's hard to put a price on that.

Job 19

The One My Grandmother Would've Been Proud Of

> **I don't like work—no man does—but I like what is in the work—the chance to find yourself. Your own reality—for yourself not for others—what no other man can ever know. They can only see the mere show, and never can tell what it really means.**
>
> Joseph Conrad, *Heart of Darkness*

I started my job at the storied news organization that liked *Shameless Acquisition Target* fifteen days after my maternal grandmother died at ninety-six.

Nana Mayer, a small Irish woman who colored her hair a deep red until eighty, would blow into Glencoe, Illinois, in her blue Oldsmobile bearing orange Tic Tacs and promising trips to McDonald's. She loved nothing more than a hamburger. The state took away her driver's license at ninety. She spent her last driving day flying up and down the expressway near her small town of Palos Park, Illinois.

For as long as I knew her, she woke up every morning to go to an eggshell-blue chair in her kitchen where she'd pick up her phone and go down a list, making five-minute calls to almost everyone she knew.

The woman was tapped in and fearless. Once, when I was an intern at WBEZ in Chicago, she was with her two sisters on Navy Pier—the "three Nanas," they called themselves. She managed to sweet-talk the longtime receptionist and made her way to my desk. I had just hung up the phone with the receptionist when, right behind me, stood the three Nanas, now all with identical duck puffs of soft white hair.

"We wanted to see where you worked, Lolo." That was her nickname for me—Lolo. The only nickname that's ever stuck.

Nana Mayer was fresh in my mind when I walked into the storied news organization that hired me in January 2023. She never quite understood what her eldest granddaughter did for a living. She certainly never quite trusted the internet. But linear television and radio she understood, as well as certain celebrated news anchors who she watched every day and who worked at the storied company where I now claimed an office. She would've been excited for me, even if she misunderstood my assigned task.

My title was executive producer for podcast programming.

Despite the gonzo nature of *Shameless Acquisition Target*, I had been chosen for this executive role based on my reputation as an honest broker and, more important, as someone who had been working professionally in podcasting for as long as one could work professionally in podcasting. And *Shameless* certainly demonstrated my thirst for success.

In my second week I got my executive headshot taken. I brought my makeup case.

The makeup artist looked at it and said, "We won't be using any of that." He got to work on my adult acne with the good stuff: television makeup.

My hair was curled, framing my face, as if to say, *Look at this painting we spackled and restored!* I wore a teal-blue suit. The resulting photo shows a steely-eyed woman with a strong jaw and a slight smile.

"Someone will look at that photo someday and think, *Look at that handsome woman*, and then give you a promotion," Danny told me.

My title was a step down, which hit my LinkedIn ego hard. My salary was significantly less than what I had calculated I could make freelancing in a year. But I found that I didn't have the guts to work for myself. At least not long-term, at least not then. Plus, I missed working with people. I'd grown feral in Brooklyn during COVID.

This is to say, it was the right job at the right time, and I took it. Plus, I thought, days after her funeral when I formally accepted the job, "Nana Mayer would've been proud."

Job 20

Dressing for the Job I Have

> **Vain trifles as they seem, clothes have, they say, more important offices than merely to keep us warm. They change our view of the world and the world's view of us . . .**
>
> Virginia Woolf, *Orlando*

I am incredibly concerned with my appearance. In part because when you grow up without money in a rich town, it's hard not to worry about how you present yourself. I also grew up with a twin brother who has the same face as me. Let me say, he is a beautiful man. But I've never been sure how this face translates to me. Kids make fun of each other, that's their trade. My twin brother's friends used to call me

"Femme Bob," as in "Femmebot," from *Austin Powers*. Austin Powers, to a child born in the eighties, is *Rebel Without a Cause* to anyone born between 1940 and 1965. For the record, my twin brother's name is not Bob, but if you hang around the Midwest long enough, people will start calling you Bob.

I couldn't control my face. But I could control my clothes and grooming. Enter a lifelong obsession with both window dressings.

Working at the storied news organization, after years of relative isolation from COVID lockdown and skittering around South Brooklyn in Crocs and overalls, kicked this obsession into overdrive. There were practical matters to consider: I did not own any pants that fit me. I needed to own pants. But, also, there were impractical matters to consider. Namely, how could I buy and groom myself into someone who looks like they work at this storied news organization? Enter me buying just *so many* blazers on the internet.

Blazers, a garment meant to pull together any outfit. They filled the hallways at my new job. An armor for the working person. I'd stare at someone in line at the Starbucks at work and imagine how well they had their shit together: Their meeting schedules were managed, they have the word *president* somewhere in their title, they have neither wrinkles nor pimples, and they don't use a glorified dog-shock-collar Pavlok wrist blaster to get out of bed in the morning.

When I wear a blazer, however, I look like I'm about to audit you.

You know how some types of clothing just don't hang right? Maybe you're someone who doesn't love a skirt, or a dress, or can't stand jeans of any cut? Blazers look like costumes on me. They show the heavy effort I'm always trying (in vain, especially as you read this book detailing all my efforts) to hide. And yet, when I'm scrolling to soothe, to blazers I go.

I've wasted hours of my life, and many hundreds of dollars, browsing online and buying clothes that weren't meant for the life I lead but rather the corporate life I've contorted myself into. A paper doll I design and dress as a way to feel a sense of control over how I want to appear to others: useful, authoritative, in control. I've tried to put an end to this coping mechanism throughout my life, but it has stayed with me.

Instead of, say, speaking to my long-term therapist about this, I did the next most rational thing: I found a hypnotist on the internet to hypnotize me out of searching for and buying blazers online.

* * *

I found the hypnotist via my friend Karen, who mentioned that her daycare mom friend's sister had recently become certified in hypnotherapy. My friend's daycare mom friend's mom's sister is named Kaveri Gautam.

All of our interactions happened over Instagram direct message, text message, Venmo, and Zoom. Kaveri said a single-minded topic/goal is always best for hypnotherapy. I felt like I was in good hands, as browsing and buying blazers on the internet was, I'd determined, certainly single-minded.

The package, which cost $160, consisted of two parts. The first, a Zoom hypnotism session in which Kaveri would do live hypnotherapy and ask me questions related to my goal. After that, Kaveri would send a personalized recording for me to listen to at least five times a week, for two weeks.

So here's the thing: I definitely wanted to stop wasting time browsing and buying blazers on the internet. But I also was not totally sure hypnotism was going to go deep enough to get me there. I've been in talk therapy for ten years, earning a PhD in "my mother." I've been in support groups. I regularly see a psychiatrist. I'm still "like this" despite all my attempts to change. I was skeptical, given the lengths I've gone to-date, that we'd get anywhere in a thirty-minute session with a follow-up audio file.

And yet, I still Venmo'd half of the $160 to secure my slot.

I scheduled the hypnotism session between meetings, with thirty-minute buffers. The buffers were meant to prepare and, potentially, recover from being hypnotized. I considered this my long lunch break.

I logged on to Zoom from my personal laptop. Kaveri joined. She's beautiful and youthful—easily ten years younger than me but with the gravity of someone who seems to *know things*. Her voice is incredibly smooth, soothing. She asked me to put on my noise-canceling headphones to block out distractions while listening to her during the session. Then, we got to it.

"Go ahead and keep your eyes closed. And as you focus on the blankness before your eyes, take a nice deep breath."

The blankness before my eyes has never been something I've given much thought to outside of getting eyelash extensions and freaking out when I realized my eyes were taped shut. A deep breath, though, I could do.

"That's right," she said. "That's right" would be an ASMR-y punctuation used throughout the session.

"Notice how your eyes want to remain this deeply relaxed. Even if you really test them, they just stay closed."

I found this to be true, and surprising. My skepticism began wavering. Kaveri continued.

"Imagine taking a step down on your perfect staircase. It could be made of clouds and in the sky, or it could be on a beach surrounded by sand and trees." She asked me what my perfect staircase looked like.

I said, "Enclosed, with wooden stairs and a white wall next to it." Not exactly clouds in the sky or on a beach. But I do dream of a home, with a staircase and a banister.

There was a long silence, and then Kaveri continued: "As you stand at the top of the staircase, you know that once you reach the bottom, you'll be transported to a place you love. It can be a place you visited, a place you have only seen, or a place that you have only ever dreamed of." She asked me to conjure a place of peace.

I said, my voice sounding and feeling heavy: "My bedroom on a weekend afternoon, with my cat Hector and a giant jug of cold water. And I'm about to take a nap."

My dreams return to sleep. Sleep and hydration. Sleep, hydration, and my elderly cat, who has been with me since I was twenty-five years old. Hector, the wise old tabby, who ignores everyone during the day but sleeps with me like a baby every night.

We continued. She asked me to imagine a doorway, offering that it could be a "grand wrought iron door." She asked me to describe my ideal doorway.

I said: "A wooden door with a round handle."

We have a saying in my household: "You must respect the wood," a bastardization of a quote from *Curb Your Enthusiasm*. Danny's grandfather was a master carpenter. The genetic preoccupation with wood respect has proven strong, forcing Danny to shove a coaster underneath anything that so much as looks like it may cause condensation. Once, I put my legs up on a wooden coffee table and I saw him think about putting a coaster underneath my foot.

At this point in the session, I was to meet someone on the other side of my wooden door with a round handle.

"As you reach out your hand, reaching toward the door, you recognize the safe, supportive energy. What would you name this energy?"

Caught off guard and suddenly more conscious than before, I said: "Uh, Rachel?" Thinking of one of my more responsible friends, who talked me down after the disastrous meeting with the popular podcast cohosts, the podcast lawyer, and the talent agent.

Kaveri dug deeper, asking me further questions about "Rachel," about my troubled childhood, and about what this energy behind the door is meant to do for me.

I said, "To help me. She's the Helper."

Kaveri said, "That's right."

Kaveri continued: "On the other side of the door is your helper, the one who's been there since you were little. The one you recently reconnected with. Previously, they thought you needed protection. They wanted to make sure you were distracted from what would hurt you, to help you fit in. But since your conversation, the Helper knows that you no longer need protecting. Instead, it is your time that needs protecting. As you push the door fully open, you see the Helper standing straight with a clipboard, determined to support you in your writing and all other creative endeavors."

Well, damn.

"Take a moment to appreciate the Helper for being the engine behind all the work you want to do. All the work you love to do. And take a moment to appreciate the fact that you and the Helper are a good team. Now allow yourself to fill up with feelings of pride as you realize that, with the Helper, you've identified the underlying reasons behind all that time, attention, and energy you put toward online browsing and shopping for blazers."

Let me reset the scene here: It's the middle of the day, I am in full business casual—I wore a blazer for the occasion; it only seemed appropriate. I'm wearing giant noise-canceling headphones, as much makeup as I ever do, and I am crying quietly, my eyes unable to open. I am crying about buying blazers on the internet. At this point in the session, I am not skeptical at all.

"Together, you and the Helper have understood that browsing and shopping were simply physical manifestations of your own desire to look past the difficulties at home and to fit in with the people outside of it."

The whole exercise was ridiculous on paper. But in under thirty minutes Kaveri articulated the underlying reason behind my soothing, if unhelpful, pastime. One hundred and sixty dollars for a one-shot fixer-up, you know I'll take it.

Kaveri began finishing the session: "Repeat: 'I direct my time, energy, and attention to the work that matters. I no longer need protection. The Helper and I focus that energy on protecting my time.'"

She then "counted me back up," meaning she brought me out of this hypnotic state. And then I wiped my eyes and returned to work.

After the hypnotism session ended, I felt refreshed. And surprised that I got so into what I would normally consider mumbo jumbo. Kaveri said I seemed "more aware" than most of her clients. That awareness probably came through with my bleakly realistic description of a stairway, a fairly normal door, and blurting out the name "Rachel" when she asked me to identify the figure behind the door.

A few days later, Kaveri sent me the audio recording, instructing me to listen to the twenty-minute recording five times a week for at least two weeks. I decided to listen to the hypnotic meditation in the early-morning hours, post Pavlok, when I was most tempted to return to scouring for blazers.

My new routine for two weeks became: get shocked out of bed via the Pavlok, feed my cats, pour myself a cup of coffee, and start the meditation. When I first listened to the recording I . . . fell asleep. Just dead-to-the-world, drool-on-my-face, head-down-on-the-sofa asleep. Turns out, this happened every single time I listened to the hypnotic meditation, even when I tried to keep my eyes wide open to the point that they became so dry that tears would run down my face.

On each of these mornings I awoke to Joanna yelling, predictably, "MOMMY. MY LITTLE HANDS ARE TOO LITTLE TO OPEN THIS BABY GATE."

Then, I'd go get her, explaining to her I was sleeping. As she asked me why, my mind would blast into consciousness. And into my frantic day.

I haven't bought a blazer since I was hypnotized. But that might be because I was asleep.

Job 21

Manifestation

> **Writing before dawn began as a necessity—I had small children when I first began to write and I needed to use the time before they said, Mama—and that was always around five in the morning.**
>
> Toni Morrison, interview in *The Paris Review*

I got Joanna a dollhouse. A beautiful, pastel dollhouse. She's three and a half and doesn't give a shit about the dollhouse, unless she suspects that one of the cats is "touching [her] stuff." But I give a shit about the dollhouse. I have given many, many shits about this dollhouse, since before she was born. Let me explain.

When I was pregnant, I read the first genetic testing report by myself in the bathroom on Thanksgiving 2020. I found out I was having a girl. One of my very first thoughts was, *Hell yes. We're gonna get a dollhouse.*

I always wanted a dollhouse when I was a child. I don't know why I never had a dollhouse, other than they can be expensive and take up a lot of space. Being small and cheap were prized qualities during my youth. It must've stuck with me because my first conscious parental projection onto Joanna was that of tiny homeownership.

When Joanna turned three, I started looking for contenders. I had some requirements: I wanted an old-fashioned wooden dollhouse. Having no handiness of my own, I determined I'd need to buy a prefabricated dollhouse. I did not want one that had been owned by someone else because that structure would be haunted. You can't buy a dollhouse from someone and expect it not to house a ghost. And I planned to put my own celestial stink on it, thank you very much.

The dollhouse needed to be wood. When I was growing up, all the toys were plastic. As a parent with an Instagram account today, you're flooded with images of wood. Wooden Montessori beds. Wooden play kitchens. Wooden play tools. Wooden play stools. Someone call Jesus, because we need a carpenter.

And finally, I wanted a nice dollhouse. A brand-name dollhouse. Assuming, as I did then, that my child would care deeply about her dollhouse, I wanted her to be proud of its origins. I scoured the sales section of different dollhouseries looking for the big, discounted win.

There's a company called Tender Leaf Toys that makes a lot of expensive wooden objects. As soon as I began inspecting the dollhouses—the Hummingbird House, the Foxtail Villa, the Dovetail House—I knew Tender Leaf was my brand. The most expensive offering? The Mulberry Mansion. For $700 you get "beautiful contemporary soft colours and detailed illustrations. . . . [A] gabled roof and attic space, opening shutters and front door with windows at the back panel," which "allow light to flood into the spacious interior." What's more, "access to a balcony on the second floor gives extra interest and space to play." It weighs 58.3 pounds, and the height reaches my chin. Its width would reach across my bosom. I pored over the Mulberry Mansion. How could I freely spend $700 on a sixty-pound, bosom-width wooden dollhouse? Where could I put such a masterful monstrosity in our small apartment? That final question made me realize that Joanna would never have the Mulberry Mansion. I didn't have the money, either, but money is fungible—I could find ways to scrape money from the walls to throw at my dreams. Space, in Brooklyn, is finite.

On the opposite end of the Tender Leaf Toys dollhouse catalog, in terms of size and price, is the Cottontail Cottage, a "delightful countryside cottage with a natural wood roof, shutters, cut out windows and space in the attic to make a bedroom. Includes a retro style set of furniture." The Cottontail Cottage is the quaint weekend retreat for residents of the Mulberry Mansion. As its name suggests, it's a home literally meant for rabbits. At full freight it costs $180 (I paid $120). It weighs 10.54 pounds. It's as tall as my knee and as wide as my femur—without a tape measure I had to use the tools at my disposal (my body). I knew just the spot where I'd put it: in front of our living room/kitchen storage cabinet where we'd narrowly miss stubbing our toes every time we passed it.

The dollhouse arrived. Danny and Joanna were, uncharacteristically, both out of the apartment. I found the toolbox and decided that it was right for me, her mother, to build (assemble) the dollhouse with my own two hands. I spent an hour in a state of confusion, counting bits of wood and screws and trying to figure out how a drill worked. In the end I took a picture of all the pieces and texted Danny:

"I bought Joanna a dollhouse. I tried to put it together. Can you please put it together?"

"This is why you're the architect and I'm the builder," he responded, a more and more common refrain as we get further into our marriage and parenthood. I come up with the ideas. Danny executes. Seems like a better deal for me.

I came home from wherever I was supposed to be when I was trying to build the dollhouse (work, probably) and surveyed the Cottontail Cottage. It was quaint and beautiful and perfect. The size was just right for our living room—just obtrusive enough to make it feel like Charlie Kaufman started building a small village in front of our couch. I set up the one scene of furniture in the dollhouse, opened and closed the front of the structure to make sure I'd placed the tiny kitchen or the tiny bed just right. And then I waited for Joanna to come home from school.

Danny wheeled our King Baby (a term I use for these giant-seeming kids still in strollers in NYC) into the kitchen, in full view of the dollhouse. She unbuckled herself (if you can unbuckle yourself from your own stroller, are you too old to use a stroller?), threw off her shoes, and walked right past the dollhouse to the couch.

"Look, Joanna, I got you a dollhouse!" I said.

Joanna squirmed over from the couch after much prodding from Danny. She looked at the front, at the sides, at the gabled roof. I opened the house to show her how she could play with it. One of our cats walked in and sniffed the toy.

"Why Pruney messing with MY STUFF?!" she shouted. Then, she chased the cat out of the room.

That's about as much attention as Joanna has paid to that dollhouse.

But not me. I'm not finished with it. If I can't have my own (Gray) house, my daughter will have the best little dollhouse she (never) imagined. It now generally sits on the filing cabinet next to my home desk. An appropriate resting place . . . for now.

卌 卌 卌 卌 ||

Job 22
Working Mother

For my daughter Kathleen who will enter the workforce in the mid-1980s prepared to accept nothing less than fully vested citizenship in the American economy.

Betty Lehan Harragan, the dedication from *Games Mother Never Taught You*

Ever since I plunged into my new job and began writing this book, my daughter and I started playing a particular game. It's called "Mommy Workin'." Joanna, three and a half years old, named the game. It goes like this: I sit at my laptop wearing my cat-eye glasses (this is precisely what I am doing right now). Joanna sits next to me with a disconnected keyboard and a wireless mouse. She's also wearing (nonprescription) cat-eye glasses. I sit and type on my laptop. Joanna sits and "types," primarily "emails." She talks out loud as she types her emails. This morning she narrated the following email: "'Dear boss. Yes. I did the work and I love you.'"

Joanna seems to think that Mommy and "Mommy Workin'" are forever interlinked. When she strolls by the office space where I rent a desk (one of my three desks: apartment desk,

Brooklyn desk rental, Manhattan job desk), she'll turn to whichever one of her friends she's with and say, "Well, my mommy works in that blue house, so." The *so* indicates pride, perhaps. But, in my lower moments, I hear it as an excuse as to why I'm not with her at the playground. Many people, often without children, tell me that someday Joanna will think about how much her mom worked and be inspired by it. That she'll recognize how much work I did for her, to help her have a better life. But, boy, does it not feel like that most of the time.

I tell Joanna that her job is to play. It's a mantra I say repeatedly, every morning. I stole this idea from, where else, Instagram. From one of the many Montessori-tinged, aesthetically-pleasing-wooden-toy parenting lifestyle accounts that explode from my "explore page," taunting me between infographics on how to organize my Outlook calendar for maximum efficiency.

She'll say, "My work is school?"

It's basically daycare, but yes.

"I go to my office at school?"

And I say yes, in a manner of speaking.

Then the pictures of Joanna start rolling onto the Brightwheel daycare messaging app (I call my Apple Watch my Brightwheel First Alert), showing her zeroed-in, deadly focused on one activity or another: seriously looking at a book alone in a wooden boat; seriously coloring a piece of paper, her hand in a tight fist, the crayon crumbling its color across the white paper; or seriously "reading" to her fellow classmates, a picture book facing outward, pretending to be her teacher. I look at these photos as I sit at one of my three desks and worry about the seriousness with which she takes her work, a.k.a. play. How much of this seriousness is innate to Joanna? How much is learned from her mother, me, workin'? Will she have trouble letting go of work as an existential tether, or will she break the cycle and chill the hell out?

* * *

Betty Lehan Harragan

I don't know how I came across the book *Games Mother Never Taught You: Corporate Gamesmanship for Women*, but I did. The title was appealing to me, for one, as my mother didn't teach me any games related to corporate gamesmanship or otherwise. Plus, I'm always looking to add to my work self-help collection. I bought it online. When it arrived—yellowed and gnarled by time and wherever it was kept—I put it in my freezer for three days to make sure any bugs in it were killed. I've dealt with bedbugs before not going to do it again. Even for this book.

I purchased it in February 2023, right after I started working at the storied news organization. *Games Mother Never Taught You*, published in 1977, was my antidote to leaning in, the Windexing of glass ceilings, the rising, the grinding, the girlbossing, the microdosing, and the cold-plunging in modern-day corporate-success manuals. Instead of inspiration, you get directives in *Games Mother Never Taught You*. It's a handbook for how to achieve the most power possible as a woman within the corporate world.

The book is made up of 120 short chapters, all with direct tactical advice, often in the titles of the chapters themselves. Some examples: "Overview of the Master Game Board," "Secrets of Success They Don't Want You to Know," "Scramble Your Signals to Protect Your Plans," "Blasting Out of the Secretarial Sand Trap," "Quarterbacking—Taking Control of a Managerial Position."

Betty Lehan Harragan writes that work is war, literally

tracing management structures to the "mightiest military machine of all time (World War II)." She continues the metaphor throughout the book, cautioning that "women's assault on the bastions of corporate power must be deflected if men are to retain their traditional authority positions." Betty is refreshingly devoid of BS.

The book is, though, a true time capsule of the late seventies, with chapters like: "Telephone Manners—a Whole New Set of Rules," "Capitalize on Sex Stereotypes," "Locker Room Language: 80% Sex, 20% Excetera," and "Company Policies on Getting Laid." There's extensive space devoted to why women shouldn't bring their purses to meetings.

The author, Betty Lehan Harragan, was a workingwoman—an executive on Madison Avenue. I imagined her sitting down to her typewriter after work and shooting out a chapter a day, drink in one hand, cigarette in the other, her third set of hands typing. There's so much of her in this book, but there's so much of her that's missing. In those early days of my new job, I found myself thinking about who Betty Lehan Harragan was, while paging through the book on my commute into the office. Then, one day, I thought to look at the dedication page:

"For my daughter Kathleen who will enter the workforce in the mid-1980s prepared to accept nothing less than fully vested citizenship in the American economy."

It turned out my subway reveries of Betty Lehan Harragan weren't that far off: "Every night my mom would come home from work, and she would sit in her rocking chair . . . a big overstuffed, upholstered rocking chair. And she would have her drink, which was one-fifth Scotch, water, and ice," said Kathleen Harragan, Betty's daughter. "She was always at her typewriter."

I spoke with Kathleen by phone, while she was at her home outside of Boston. She's grown now, and Betty is gone. She seemed surprised to hear from me, asking how I came across her mother's work and what interested me about it.

"The clash at the center of my book," I said, "is my daughter."

Yes, I was raising my daughter while feeling the hole of my mom's absence from my own childhood. Talk to any Better-Help clinician and they will say this is a common topic. But, as ever, I found myself numbing the sadness with work. So I asked Kathleen: "How do I raise a daughter in proximity to me, a me who is always urgently fanning the flames of my résumé just in case the Olympic torch needs a light?" Too bad emailing isn't in the Games. Yet.

Basically, how did Betty do it?

Betty Lehan Harragan's dedication to Kathleen—complete with her baldly ambitious hopes for her then-young daughter—touched me. If there was someone who could understand having a mother with a résumé on fire, I suspected it was Kathleen.

Betty began writing *Games Mother Never Taught You* after a familiar catastrophe: She was fired from her job.

"One day, when I was ten years old, she came home, and she got her Scotch out of the cabinet. And she said, 'Kathleen, I have news.' I was like, 'What?' And she said, 'Today I got fired from my job.'"

"Why did they fire you?" Kathleen asked.

"Because I found out that a man who is doing the exact same job that I am doing is making way more than I am. And when I asked them why, they told me, 'He is the head of household and has a family to support.' And I said, 'I have a child to support.' And they said 'That doesn't matter. He is the head of household, so he should make more money.' So I'm going to take them to court, and they don't like that."

Because of the lawsuit, Betty was "blackballed," to use Kathleen's word, from other high-paying jobs on Madison Avenue. Betty got involved with the National Organization for Women (NOW) for assistance with her case, to get consulting jobs via connections from NOW, and later for research for her book. Kathleen went along with her mother back then in the 1980s to the NOW meetings in the Village, doing her homework in the building's lobby. NOW lawyers working pro bono on Betty's case would come over to the Harragan's apartment, with their own typewriters, clacking and smoking while preparing briefs. Kathleen remembers that in the morning, all the women would be in the same clothes they were in the day before. They worked through the night.

In middle school Betty handed Kathleen a document.

"She told me that she was going to write a book. And here

was the outline. And I remember looking at the outline, and I was like, 'I don't understand any of these words.'" Then Kathleen went back to her business. The business of being a kid.

Betty wrote the book while Kathleen was in middle school. It was published when Kathleen was in high school. Meanwhile, Betty was using her large Rolodex and expertise to help Kathleen launch into her own career.

For example, Kathleen didn't personally choose to go to Bronx High School of Science—an incredibly competitive public high school in New York City—but Betty had her walking in the doors for her first day based on the strength of Kathleen's test scores. Then Betty convinced Kathleen to apply to MIT after reading a news report about MIT's interest in admitting more women. Kathleen didn't want to apply to MIT.

When Kathleen came home to a thick admissions envelope from MIT on the table, she turned to her mom and said: "We're about to have a fight, aren't we?"

"Yes, we are," Betty said.

Kathleen ended up going to MIT but had a hard time adjusting to school.

"When [my mother] died, I got a sympathy card from the woman who was the dean of student affairs at MIT the years I was there. I didn't know her. And this sympathy card was like 'Your mother was such a force. I so enjoyed my time spent with her.' And I was like, 'What the hell?'

"And then, my mother being a writer, she kept journals. After she died . . . I sat down for weeks and just read through all her journals. And in her journals, she journaled about how she was so worried about me at MIT because of my mental health. I was saying 'I'm going to quit college; I don't belong here.' And how she got connected to the dean of student affairs, I think maybe because she was the first woman dean at MIT; maybe she'd read my mom's book and that was the connection. So she had the dean of student affairs personally watching over me when I was at MIT, and I had absolutely no idea.

"During college I would call [my mother] all the time, and she's like, 'Kathleen, you've got to stop calling me so much,'" to telegraph to Kathleen that she was independent.

"But she was pulling the strings."

Kathleen went on to graduate from MIT with a management and marketing major. She got a job at IBM fresh out of school, with Betty's encouragement. Kathleen heard about the job because her longtime childhood neighbor worked at the company. She initially moved back in with Betty (which, Kathleen speculates, was probably part of the appeal of the IBM job for Betty). After years at IBM and other companies, Kathleen—the fully vested member of the American economy—had a conflict.

"Everyone always said, 'Find what you love and then figure out how to make money at it.' I just never found what I loved."

When Kathleen got pregnant, she decided she wanted to stay home with her child. "If I do this job right, then I will absolutely make a difference to somebody. And that somebody may just be my child," she thought. But she dreaded telling Betty, given all the work she'd done—with *Games Mother Never Taught You*, her tireless fight for women's rights in the workplace, and her many business accomplishments.

"And she said, 'Kathleen, what we all fought for was for you to have the choice. And if you want to make your choice to stay home with your child, that's also what we fought for.' And that just lifted all the guilt."

Throughout our conversation I kept rounding back to the same themes with Kathleen. Namely, how can I be a good working example to my daughter without making her think work is all that matters to me, or to the world? How to stop the "Mommy Workin'" game from turning into "Mommy is always at work and unavailable to me"?

Kathleen told me, "The only constant was my relationship with my mother. She was always there. My memory is that my mom was always at the keyboard. That's where she loved being. That's where she belongs. It's not a bad memory at all. That was her work."

Always there. Always at the keyboard. Sounds familiar.

Job 23

Moving On Up

> **The clothes smell fresh, look bright and clean,
> the family verdict—quote supreme.**
>
> Advertisement for Fab laundry detergent in the 1960s

As you've perhaps realized, my idea of "making it" is owning a home. Ideally a home I think is nice. One with a foundation that doesn't sink too much. One with a garage I can turn into my personal work lair. One with a yard where my daughter can train her cat to walk on a leash.

A more realistic mark of "making it" in my rent-controlled apartment, particularly as we tried and failed to potty train Joanna, was having an in-unit washer and dryer.

Danny and I have lived under the same landlord, in two different rent-stabilized buildings, in Brooklyn for seven years. When we moved in, we were simply escaping pestilence: bedbugs at a prior apartment. (We spent thousands of dollars to have odorless gas kill anything living in any of our things in a specialized moving truck. I've since noticed that the unit underneath our bedbug apartment is now a commercial office: a bedbug abatement outfit. Poetic.)

We've gotten comfortable here. When we moved across the street, from an apartment with one and a half bedrooms to a three-bedroom, we got a dishwasher, a couch, an actual bed instead of a foam pad on the floor. Even a Peloton decorates the darkest corner near the less attractive of two cat scratchers. All of this marks our arrival at the waiting room to stability, upward mobility, maturity. And if not for the many miniature undies that require regular laundering, today, I might be satisfied.

Joanna's arrival puts us at six loads of laundry a week, all done in the coin-operated laundry machines, which are two floors below, in the lobby of the building. Joanna enjoys throwing out the "yuck," otherwise known as the lint, when we clean out each of the dryers before and after we use them. But, after dragging all of our laundry, and Joanna, up and down the stairs too many times to count, in 2024 I decided it was time to make securing our own washer and dryer a job.

I drafted an email for Danny to send to our landlords, Lenny and Igor (men tend to respond better to men asking for things—*I know*—but I figured I gotta work the system I got). It acknowledged facts I'd picked up about Igor (he has twins), and facts I knew Lenny also knew (we pay our rent six days before its due; Danny has single-handedly saved tens of thousands of dollars for the landlords by finding and reporting water damage over the years).

Danny read the email.

"Why do any of these details matter?" he said.

"We have to leverage our knowledge and also make it clear to them that letting us have a washing machine will cost them less than losing us as tenants," I said.

Danny dutifully sent the email to Lenny and Igor.

One hour later, Lenny responded. Igor would come by to talk about installation plans the next day. Sure enough, Igor showed, along with our beloved super. They would buy the washer/dryer. They would install it. It would be done within the next two weeks. If you've lived in New York or any urban area without washer/dryers in-unit, you'll understand why I yelped in shocked disbelief when we got the reply. I put the accomplishment on my LinkedIn profile.

Two weeks later, we had the washer/dryer. I ran one load of tiny, soiled underpants (not mine). I folded those clothes as soon as they finished drying. And then—wait for this one—I put them away. My Sunday very-early mornings (I would often blast myself awake at 5:00 a.m. to beat the Sunday wash rush) would no longer be spent surrounded by "laundry mountain," otherwise known as six loads of all our family's cloth possessions. I now know a (type of) peace.

Job 24

I Live a Double Life

The opposite of play isn't work. It's depression.

Brian Sutton-Smith, play theorist

At night, Danny and I put Joanna to bed. We brush her teeth. We read her two books. Afterward, I stay in Joanna's bed to tell her stories about her orange stuffed cat, named Cookie. Those stories used to involve Cookie going to the supermarket. Or to the library, where he has a job "stacking books." Or, a crowd-pleaser, Cookie going to Nonni's house in Staten Island. Cookie's central obsession is Joanna. But, in the stories, he's always on the prowl in the neighborhood. Lately, Cookie's activities have expanded. He's now writing a book about his life: *Cookie Himself* by

Cookie Himself. Of course, Joanna is his main subject, since he is always at Joanna's side.

This story came to me in part because I wanted Joanna to understand why I spend so much time away, working on this book or working at my job. Children, famously, like hearing the same stories over and over again. And Cookie's book has really caught on. I've had to expand the details and the scope of Cookie's work. Cookie writes every day about Joanna. When he needs inspiration for his writing, he stops his work and goes on various walks: to the supermarket, the subway, or the Little Cupcake Bakeshop, to gather material about Joanna. He now has a best fantasy friend, a human man named Ned. Ned runs the Little Cupcake Bakeshop and helps Cookie get out of scrapes.

Cookie must've finished his book (we haven't gotten into the details of how he finished the book, as I haven't yet finished this book). Cookie has been holding large readings, which many adoring cat fans attend. Joanna goes to every reading and stands just offstage, to look at Cookie and the crowd. Sometimes our actual cats—Hector, Lulu, and Pruney—surprise Cookie by sitting in the audience. Cookie may have one book to promote, but he's always working on another. A light determination driving him, yes, but mainly his curiosity about Joanna's life. His next book? *How the Cookie Crumbles* by Cookie Himself.

I recently realized that I am deeply jealous of my own creation: the alter ego of my daughter's stuffed cat.

Catch me on a Monday morning and I am, as my friend Kate said, "disturbingly corporate." Hair straightened, my short bob clipped behind my ears. Makeup on. Fake eyelashes brushed. Leather bag on my shoulder. I often wear monochromatic black or navy outfits and my one pair of nice shoes (I bought a pair of Gucci loafers the day I stopped working at the Big Entertainment Money company—don't take financial advice from me). I commute 60 to 110 minutes from my neighborhood in Brooklyn to the Upper West Side. I sit at a desk and type, minding my posture. I try to appear prim and poised in meetings, even as I roil against playing corporate pretend. I hold my tongue and stay in my lane—most of the time. At these times, I think to myself, *I am playing a role: "Mommy Workin'."*

When Mommy comes back home, she kicks off those Gucci loafers, and she (I) start(s) obsessing over small bits of gossip or intrigue or friction that stuck to me during the day. Poor Danny has the sincere pleasure of listening to all of it. Joanna definitely overhears bits and pieces of my dread.

Meanwhile, Cookie has spent the early morning at his tiny desk, with his tiny laptop, and a tiny cup of water, which he puts on a separate, lower surface so as not to spill water on his laptop. He writes in the mornings—with inspiration from sleeping in Joanna's bed fresh in his mind (Cookie is also able to access Joanna's dreams, another capability I'm jealous of). And then, in the early afternoon, he leaves the house in search of insight on, or cupcakes for, Joanna. He may put on his big yellow hat, his big yellow coat, and his big yellow shoes, and walk to Target to see about some squeezy ball toy Joanna talks about. On the way, he'll run into his friends Tulip and Petunia—two pink cats who happen to be a mother and daughter duo. They'll have small talk. And then, Cookie continues on his way.

When he arrives at Target, he takes time to touch all the toys (as Joanna does) and then finds the yellow squeezy ball. He squeezes it and looks at the price: five dollars. That's convenient because Cookie always has exactly $5 on him, from his part-time job stacking books at the library. He buys the squeezy ball and tromps back home, just in time to see Daddy and Joanna return from school. It's then that he gives Joanna the squeezy ball, they play together, and Cookie gathers more inspiration for his future book. Mommy is telling these stories but is absent from them, because "she's WORKIN'."

On nights and weekends I do my best impersonation of Cookie. I put on my big blue baseball cap that has *LC* on it. The *LC* is not for a sports team, it's for *La Colombe*, the company that makes my cold brew cans of choice. Danny finds canned coffee consumed at home wasteful. I bought the hat to lightly spite him and now wear it every non–storied news organization workday.

Last year Joanna wore exclusively black velour dresses and a red bow headband from her favorite film, *Kiki's Delivery Service*. Kiki is a teenage witch who leaves home for the first time, finds purpose, and finds friendship and love (as does her pet cat, Gigi). Joanna would ask her daycare teacher to fly her around on a toy broom. Joanna became known around town as the blond girl in the red-bow headband. To commemorate her first obsession, I recently got a fairly large tattoo on my arm of Joanna's iconic *Kiki's Delivery Service* red-bow headband. I showed a photo of the tattoo to my dad, and he said, "It looks like a bikini top." That tattoo is loud and proud when I'm not at work. I go to yoga, take my Chaturangas seriously, and stick around to overhear the studio gossip. When Joanna sees the tattoo, I remind her that I put something permanent on my body to carry a bit of her with me wherever I go.

I take my time walking from yoga to my writing desk (the desk where I wrote the *Shameless* podcast, which does not have a separate, lower surface for beverages), stopping my walking to peep at houses, or to chat with other parents I run into on the main drag. I leisurely take the temperature of the neighborhood.

I'll go to my rented desk, write this book for several hours, then return to Joanna and Danny, both of whom are often caked in Kinetic Sand, paint, or dirt after a day of rolling around in all three. I'll look at Joanna and marvel. She's three and a half and therefore occasionally a pain in the ass, but she learns something new every day. She is, ruthlessly, alive. She's at an age where she can't help but be completely herself at all times. I see why Cookie focuses his work on her.

If you've gotten this far and not thought *Perhaps this woman needs to be committed,* I applaud you for your open mind and industrious thinking.

Perhaps you find other ways to compartmentalize your life—perhaps ways that are not impersonating your daughter's stuffed animal on nights and weekends. I want to learn from people like you. How does one sit and act one way in a work setting and then take on a totally different role during the rest of their life? What kind of metaphorical Container Store do I need to go to in order to keep the two halves of my lives separated? How do I stop the roil? How do I stop feeling trapped between who I want to be—my daughter's stuffed orange cat, Cookie—and who I feel like I am for sixty-plus hours a week: a LinkedIn profile with a panic disorder?

My job sounds impressive. A lot of people have watched *The Morning Show* on Apple TV and will often say, "So your job is like that?"

No, no, my job is not like that, for blessed reasons (I don't know how to run a television show; I only recently discovered the difference between concealer and foundation) and for cursed ones (it can feel more like *The Mourning Show*, for me, at least).

"Mommy works for [famous cartoon character]," Joanna says, due to an oversimplified explanation by me of how parent companies work to a three-and-a-half-year-old (the storied news organization is owned by an even more storied entertainment company).

Cookie himself helps me. When feeling frustrated and stuck at work, I soothe myself by dropping into my alter ego: Writer Cookie. A part-time job, small errands and conversations, with the energy to sit at a tiny computer to write and the space to just be.

I don't think I've ever known that space. I've always kept running, kept stuffing more into my life. Because, as a kid, to succeed was to survive. As a middle-aged woman I'm still in that kid logic, too.

* * *

In the *Shameless* podcast I explained a type of unofficial job I've held inside companies—I called it "corporate mommy." This is a job I warn listeners against taking. Here are the tenants of a corporate mommy, as described in the podcast (in song, incidentally):

Definition: *corporate mommy*: a managerial role set up to patch structural or cultural problems within a work environment . . . not to actually lead a team.

In the hiring process pay attention to the following to avoid becoming a corporate mommy:

1. Does your new role have some level of independence, decision-making wise? If not, the folks you manage will have been waiting for stuff to happen for a long time. Your position may even have been *blamed* as the reason things haven't gotten done.

2. Pay attention to the reporting structure—especially if it gives you two bosses. If so, in the interview process, find out if both of those people realize that you're reporting to both of them. That might seem obvious but . . . it's often not. Don't accidentally get in the middle of a middle-manager feud.

3. If someone else once occupied the position, pay attention to how hiring managers talk about that person in the hiring process. Ideally, they don't talk about that person at all. Any responsibility for the last version of this role not working out should be acknowledged as a problem with the role, not with an individual.

4. This is a cliché but run, don't walk, if anyone in the hiring process boasts that the company feels like "a family." You will be their mom.

5. CONSIDER IF YOU WANT TO BE IN MANAGEMENT IN THE FIRST PLACE. Moving "up" the hierarchy—and, in the case of a lot of jobs, away from doing the actual stuff that got you there in the first place—may not be the right move for you.

I circulated this list on social media, too, as "Laura Mayer's Five Point Plan for How You Can Avoid Being a Corporate Mommy," with the subtitle "Note: Laura Mayer LOVES

HAVING A JOB." I urged listeners not to take corporate mommy jobs if they didn't want them and to heed my warnings to avoid being in one. I received emails and direct messages from many people saying they had succumbed to corporate mommyhood and still do.

The subtitle, "Laura Mayer LOVES HAVING A JOB," was a giant skywriter's message to the hiring-powers-that-be that I was on the job market. The list wasn't only meant to help others. It was also meant to both (a) keep me accountable from taking corporate mommy jobs in the first place, and (b) have any savvy hiring manager realize I wouldn't be a good fit for their corporate mommy position. Smart, right?

Let me back up and say, for the record, that I harbor a lifelong love for the storied news organization where I now work.

I watched their weekly newsmagazine programs most nights, from childhood all the way until college. The only book I can remember reading during COVID lockdown was the CEO's memoir, in between deadlifts on my roof. Gotta love a weather man turned worldwide business magnate. Seriously.

But I was especially prone to taking a job given the financial straits I didn't want to end up in: that's to say, dire ones, with a child, and without job-sponsored health insurance. If I'm being honest, I knew I was going to take the job if it were offered to me as soon as the recruiter reached out.

After I got the offer, my lawyer said, "Accept in your heart that you will be in this job for four years."

I told her, too quickly, "It's accepted in my heart. It's accepted!" She knew about my restlessness.

"What if I take this job and try not to care as much about work?" I said to Danny.

"That seems like a good idea," he said.

It was a great idea. What if I just chilled out for the first time ever? Left work at work. Enjoyed my weekends? Took flexibility where I could find it? Became a company woman and an area mom?

It was a great idea, sure. But about a year into my contract, I started to feel that familiar gnaw. I wanted to do more, to fix problems, to be bigger, to make more, to cut red tape. I was no longer leaving work at work.

Here are some of the things I should've thought about before taking this perfectly fine, impressive-seeming job:

I realized how often my boss and other people would say some variation of "Good, you haven't run screaming from the building yet!" This began happening in my first week, and I laughed it off. It still happens, two years in. I was, perhaps, too fast to laugh.

And then, I looked back at an old notebook, at the copious notes I took when going through the interview process for the job. I wrote down, and I quote: "Team feels like a family." In through one ear, written on paper, and gone out the other.

𝍸𝍸𝍸𝍸𝍸

Job 25

Basket Case

> **I was seized with a feeling of loneliness, misery, and horror, as though I had been flung down against my will into this great hole full of shadows, where I was standing all alone with the belfry looking at me with its red eye.**
>
> Anton Chekhov, *Panic Fears*

As you know, I'm often angry at work. All the time. Keeping up appearances—holding my tongue, remaining poised, keeping my cool—is not a strength of mine. If I don't find a way to release this anger—say, through exercise, or ranting wildly in appropriate company, or making nonsensical jokes about the situation, or writing this book—then the anger swirls up inside of me and causes a panic attack. Panic attacks, if you haven't had the pleasure, are not fun. They're spiritual heart attacks that feel like physical ones. My mind makes me feel like I'm going to die, and I flee—mentally (to a place of calm: see blazer hypnotic meditation) or sometimes physically (slinking slowly out of conference rooms or off subway cars). When the panic attacks are strong enough, my worst reaction is feeling as if I literally don't exist. That I've evaporated and I'm watching my life from outside of myself. That's known as depersonalization/derealization. These episodes are generally brief and respond well to certain medications. But, think for a moment, about how brutally fucked-up it is that I could allow my mind to make myself feel like it doesn't exist, all because of something like a PowerPoint presentation.

Sometimes these panic attacks don't have a clear-to-me cause. I'll be sitting on the train, playing a game or listening to a podcast, and *BAM*—my heart starts racing, my hands start sweating, my eyesight grows a bit distant, and the depersonalization begins. No matter how much therapy or psychiatry I've gone through, I've yet to find a way to end these panic attacks. Frustratingly, the only way I live with them is by letting my body go through the full spiritual and physical freak-out and emerge in some type of condition on the other end, generally a sweatier one than the one I was in when I entered.

And, if I'm honest, that's been happening a lot more frequently these days.

卌 卌 卌 卌 卌 |

Job 26

Life Negotiator

> **In my experience, the words "now just calm down" almost inevitably have the opposite effect on the person you are speaking to.**
>
> Elyn R. Saks, *The Center Cannot Hold: My Journey Through Madness*

One Tuesday evening, in the second year of my contract at the storied news organization, I had another panic attack on the train on my way home from work. Something about this particular panic attack broke me. I was working on something for this book (relistening to one of my favorite memoirs), playing *Cooking Mama*, sitting down, and generally chilling. Then suddenly I felt the thick tar of panic, heavy and undulating, wash all over me. My vision blurred more than usual this time. I felt like I was going to pass out. I tore at my cuticles to try to shock myself awake and away from this episode, with no luck. I didn't time it, but this panic attack felt longer than any one I had before. And it came, to my mind, from nowhere. But, actually, from the pit where I'd stashed all of my anger, and hatred, and sorrow for this job and every job I've ever tried to do but couldn't quite fulfill. All the ideas for what I wanted my future work to be like that I stuffed down because I felt like a failure.

I sat with the panic attack for the night. I sat with my kid. I sat with my cat Hector. I told Danny. We had recently reviewed the money I'd saved from my Big Job, and though most of it was meant for retirement or other far-off plans, we had determined it was enough for me to leave my job if I absolutely needed to.

The next morning, still sore from tensing my muscles during the panic attack from the evening before, I pulled a move that always works on me: I requested a meeting with my boss and didn't specify the subject. Whenever that happens to me I know someone is about to announce that they're quitting or some other Big Problem. Foreboding. Like sending someone a text that says "Call me." This is an evil tactic that must be used sparingly.

"I'm quitting my job," I told my coworker ahead of the meeting. I felt stoic.

"Wow. Okay," he said. His tone somber but accepting. I felt

like I'd disappointed a deeply understanding dad. He even rolled up his sleeves.

And then, I did it. I walked into my boss's office—who, by the way, was the best boss I ever had (TBBIEH)—sat down on one of her chairs, and told her. "This job isn't working for me. I'm leaving. This is for personal reasons." For real this time.

Why "personal reasons"? Especially after that particular phrase had been wielded against me when leaving the podcast startup in 2015? Let's be real, if you've read this book up until now, you know the "personal reasons" are legit.

My boss moved from the chair across from me and sat on her couch, nearer to me. "I hear you. I'd hate to lose you," she said.

And then . . . I immediately started crying. Of course I started crying.

"Is there anything we can do to keep you?"

In my memory I'm holding a pillow in my lap during this meeting. I was not, in fact, holding a pillow in my lap, but you understand the general vibe.

"No," I said. And that was true.

Over the course of that meeting, TBBIEH listened to me, reasoned with me, and through some sort of corporate transmogrification, my "I quit" became "I'll think about it for a week, and then come back with a plan, if there's a plan that exists that would make the job work for me." I could continue in a different role, adjust my schedule for a time, identify a change that could keep me in the job. Something.

"Take some time off," TBBIEH said. This happened the Wednesday before Labor Day weekend.

Famously, actress Claire Danes has perfected the "ugly cry." She is beautiful and yet turns into a molting sea creature when she cries on-screen. I'm no stage beauty, so that's not the comparison here. Let's just say no one has ever thought, *You're beautiful when you cry*. My face gets swollen and red, and my eyelashes fall out at a greater clip. I've never understood that last part. I don't return to equilibrium for at least forty-five minutes.

I was in that state when I returned to my office.

"I did it," I said, to my upstanding colleague.

"Wow," he said.

And then his phone rang. It was TBBIEH calling him into her office.

With no meetings left on my schedule for the day, I decided to leave the office. I ran into someone else I work with, who was with her family. It was that odd week between summer programs ending and public school beginning, so there were a lot of kids coming to visit their parents at work. This particular coworker is similarly kind, as everyone I directly worked with was. She was, and is, uniquely maternal. If there's one person in that building who's attuned to someone who has recently cried, it's her. I did a stop-and-chat and could tell that she, both of her parents, and her two children could tell I'd recently been crying.

"Take care of yourself," she said, as I exited the building.

I got back on the panic train, this time more shocked than anything else. I'd never done something this drastic without a clear plan in place. Sure, I'd quit jobs. But that was for other jobs. And sure, there were repercussions. But, generally, I was the one who was acting rationally, calmly, not impulsively. From The Chart to this moment, I'd always understood what the "next step" should or could be. This time, I didn't.

I came home, ripped off my blouse, and fell asleep. I woke up to my alarm for a yoga class. I was not about to lose twenty-five dollars, so I bolted up from a deep sleep, put on my yoga clothes, and ran out the door as Joanna, once again, asked, "Is there a baby in there?" upon seeing my stomach in my yoga pants.

I've become a regular at the yoga studio in my neighborhood. I hadn't been doing any kind of regular exercise since I started working again in-office. But, three months prior, I'd started "practicing" (I often bristled at this phrase—in yoga you're always practicing and never "finished"—how annoying!) hot yoga. I don't consider myself suited to yoga: I don't know where my hips are in space, I'm not very flexible, and the last ten minutes or so of each class being devoted to stillness kill me.

But, there was something about being in downward dog and literally seeing my body produce sweat—watching the beads begin as liquid spots and grow into tiny pearlescent orbs before falling onto my mat; my body a literal science experiment—that kept me coming back. During the Savasana (a.k.a. the stillness portion), the period at the end of the class where you lie sweaty on your mat and rest, that night I started to lightly cry. My thoughts went from *What had I done to my family? To myself? To my career?* to *What if there's some sort of "creative solution," as my boss suggested. Maybe, this time, I don't flee?*

Leaving the class, sweaty and swollen from crying, I could tell the yoga teacher felt like she'd done her job. And dammit, she did.

The next day, my coworker texted me about his meeting with TBBIEH. Her first question to him was "How are you holding up?" She knew that he knew, and that we worked closely together. They discussed what the succession plan would look like when I left. How high could they promote someone already in a job on the team to the seemingly vaulted executive producer title? What was an interim solution? My coworker texted, asking me to weigh in on the various options. I gave him my opinion on how to best replace me, then told him, "Find a way to get yourself promoted. Get more money." Because why not?

And also: "Hold on a minute," I texted. "I might not fully leave after all."

I kept thinking *Don't flee,* after that damn Savasana. The panic, this time at least, was my discrete reason for leaving. In the past it had been ambition, which, for me, can be a form of panic in a nice suit.

I'd never had a boss, or a boss figure, absorb any of my concerns, in a real way. And I felt like TBBIEH had. I was chafing against what this all would do to the idea of me bravely leaving without a plan and figuring it all out—somehow emerging whole in the end. Honestly, I was worried about what this decision would do to this very book you're reading. The book I hadn't finished writing.

* * *

The plan? I'd work from home three days a week, therefore avoiding the panic train. I spoke to my coterie of experts (my therapist and psychiatrist), and they agreed that this light avoidance of the train wouldn't be a bad thing as I went on new medication and generally tried to figure out what was going on with my own mind. On Tuesdays and Thursdays I'd stop work at two, to tend to things related to my kid, and related to my health, but sign on again around six to close any loops that had opened while I was offline. I'd work this schedule from September through the end of the year (2024). Then, in January, TBBIEH and I would reassess.

In practice the plan has been an exercise in boundaries—the discomfort with asserting them for the first time in a work environment and the discomfort with sticking to them. I always want to bend to the needs of others when their needs are made clear to me. That's the first job I ever had, after all.

Job 1

The Only Job I Couldn't Quit

In August 2017 millions of people in America went to tiny towns to see the "Great American Eclipse." I am afraid of space and am not interested in thinking about it or discussing it, but my understanding with this particular eclipse is the moon crossed paths with the sun, making the sky totally dark during the brightest part of the day, and people like seeing that for some reason. Gives me the icks! I need my sun where I need it: unobstructed, in the sky. But seeing darkness was the hot new thing of the summer of 2017. And my father, Bob Mayer, was hell-bent on seeing "totality."

I was thirty years old, married, employed, and, by all accounts, an adult. It had been thirteen years since my mom's arrest and attempt to reframe it as a child's cry for attention. Twenty-one years since I met Mr. Coke Nail at Einstein Bros.

Bagels. While I'm sure that gentleman had moved on, my family had been maintaining a carefully tended status quo. My mom never left the house. My dad supplied her with just enough alcohol to avoid her from going into withdrawal. It was almost a scientific enabling experiment. The most standardized instability possible. Admirable control, almost.

My dad was going alone to the eclipse in Carbondale, Illinois, a seven-hour drive when you're a man who enjoys the scenic route. My mom was staying in the house alone, which she had, by that point, been doing for thirteen years straight. Save for visits from my grandmother when they'd go to restaurants, or on drives with my dad, she'd sit alone in her room and drink, and watch the news and soap operas, all while maintaining at least a Level 3. That, and my father banning her from driving, was the lasting impact of the arrest.

Twelve years earlier, my dad quietly decided to work from home full-time, to keep an eye on my mother—though he'd never admit that was the reason. He bought and brought the alcohol to the household, doled it out to her like medicine. Because, by this point, if she didn't have a certain amount of alcohol in her system, she could go into dangerous withdrawals. But neither of them were interested in addressing the problem, in seeking actual counseling, in going to a treatment center. Aside from the night of the arrest, my mother hadn't been to a doctor of any kind for thirty years.

My dad drank as well, and at times they had fun together. My dad even had his own chart. My mom would drink these gallon glass jugs of Carlo Rossi white wine. My dad took out a Sharpie and made tick marks on the jug, with headings: at the top, when less of the wine was drunk, said "Happy"; a quarter of the way down, "Sad"; halfway down, "Angry"; an inch from the bottom, "Very, very mad." That's the most he ever addressed her drinking.

My father sought out the eclipse nonsense as an attempt to touch something the alcohol could not, perhaps. He left early for Carbondale, Illinois, a long drive from where he lived, to arrive before the sky started to shift. He made some friends and sent me a photo of himself with his eclipse glasses waiting for the totality, which I received during a pitch meeting. When it was over, he went to his car to drive home.

He then got stuck in the worst traffic jam rural Illinois had seen to date. He stopped texting. He started calling, screaming. Screaming that he was going to run out of gas. Screaming that he needed to get home. Swearing. It was 10:00 p.m. EST, and I was on Hotels.com trying to find him a room. Going back and forth with him, trying to convince him to get off the road, to stop screaming, to go to sleep. I booked him a hotel room, the last in the area. He said, "Thank you," and then wouldn't respond to any of my messages. It turns out he decided to keep on going, keep on driving home to my mother. Fifteen hours in the car on a drive that usually takes seven.

Why didn't my father take a break, take the last hotel room in Middle of Nowhere, Illinois, an expensive one because of the demand, that his daughter got him after pleading with the hotel desk? Because he found out my mother was out of alcohol. And he needed to get some to her, to kill her and to save her at the same time.

Around that time, many of my dad's activities revolved around tending to and, in this case, creating life. In the winter of 2017 my dad convinced a cat breeder to knock up his favorite cat, Blondie, so he could have a litter of Burmese kittens. This involved several filmed dalliances with a purebred sire, and a lot of paperwork stating he would absolutely not create a spin-off cattery. Two weeks after the eclipse, Blondie gave birth to five kittens. One was stillborn, though my dad attempted to revive her via CPR. But it didn't work. Four kittens survived as well as Blondie, the mother, who gave birth on top of a suitcase in my old childhood bedroom.

"Having cats is better than having children," my mom slurred to me on the phone, a solid Level 4. "I never loved having kids like I do these babies."

I got videos from my dad of my parents playing with the kittens. My mom so absolutely bombed in all the videos that she couldn't pick up a kitten and put it back down gently: She'd hold one and then drop it from shoulder level, a long way to the floor.

Weeks later my uncle, my dad's brother, needed heart surgery in Indiana. The plan: My dad was going to go to Indiana for the operation, make sure his brother came out of the operation well, and then stay overnight. My dad texts me and my twin brother constantly. Of his whereabouts. Jokes.

Names for things: "Good cat name . . . Musket." He's not afraid to take a really close-up photo of a stranger he finds interesting and send it along.

On this trip, he abruptly texted my twin brother saying that he was leaving early because he left his phone charger at home. Then we didn't hear from him for hours. My twin brother kept saying he had a bad feeling about things. I, too, had a bad feeling, but this one was even badder than usual. I always have a bad feeling. But what could we do? My brother called the police to ask for a wellness check at their home. The Glencoe police officers told him that a "woman, mid-sixties, was taken by ambulance to intensive care. Cardiac unit." The clearest statement of fact about our mom that we'd ever heard.

What happened: My mother had run out of alcohol. She was at a full-awake Level 5 by noon, having drunk all the wine my dad left her within hours. Knowing she needed to get more, and wanting to keep some cover, she called a pizza place that also delivered alcohol. When the delivery driver arrived, she fell down the stairs so violently that she was unconscious. The delivery driver called 911. And then my dad came home to bring her more alcohol. But she was already at the hospital.

The doctors put my mom under heavy sedation for five days. To run tests. To detox her safely. She was in the intensive care unit. My dad spent all day in a chair next to her, texting my brother and me pictures of the "newfangled robots" that did things in the hospitals. I think they were hand sanitizer machines. On the first day, before they sedated her, she said, "Bob, we need beer for lunch."

Bob, otherwise known as my dad, tried to take her out of the hospital, concerned insurance wouldn't pay for the stay.

"If you take her out of here," the doctor said, "you will kill her."

So she stayed for a week.

All of this information came in bits and pieces. Some details given to me, others given to my twin brother. My twin brother and I came together to create a distorted puzzle of what was going on. I was focused on numbers—AST, ALT, the condition of her liver, her pancreas, her red blood cell count, her hemoglobin. Give me numbers to cling to so I can anchor myself in data.

During that week, my dad woke to the mother cat, Blondie, holding the runt of her litter in her mouth. The runt was dead, and she gave him to my father in bed.

My mother got out of the hospital a week after she went in. I was desperate to call her, to hear her clearheaded for the first time that I could remember. I was told I could call, so I did immediately, in this Buddhist-themed café near my then-job.

"I can't believe this happened. It was so scary, Laura. It just went blank."

"Blank? What do you mean."

"Never mind. I have to go." And she hung up.

She refused to talk to me for a year.

I tried calling her every other day—November to November. She never picked up. My father would pick up, and I would hang up. Then, I'd collect myself, call my dad back, and ask why my mom wouldn't speak to me. He acted as if I never asked the question and would tell me about his day.

I pieced together data from visits by my twin brother, who lived in Chicago, near enough to visit occasionally. "Things seemed weird there," my brother told me on the phone, while I was walking back from an Orangetheory class in which I was certain John Turturro was a fellow attendee.

"She seemed fine," he said another weekend.

"Was she drinking?"

"No. I think she really, actually stopped drinking this time," he said.

I never had access to her, really, at any age. But now I had virtually no insight to make my assessments—to see if she was really done drinking, to mentally, if not actually, keep The Chart that I kept as a child. She cut me off right as she'd finally done what I had always most hoped she'd do. I was sad and furious.

I received the following texts from my dad a little over a year after she detoxed:

Dad: Mom just got rolled in for surgery.

Me: What????

Dad: There's a mass.

Me: What? Where?

Dad: Colon.

A mass. The first I heard of my mom having cancer came from my dad idly texting in the hospital. Then, a picture of one of those robo-hand sanitizers. Then many photos of the cafeteria. "They've fixed it up since last year."

Earlier that week, my mom had blood taken by a new doctor. That same night, Monday night, she was called to the hospital for an abdominal MRI. Her red blood count was so low that the doctors knew there was internal bleeding somewhere. They found "the mass," the tumor. By Thursday she was in surgery, and that's when I got the text about hand sanitizer robots.

When she came back from the hospital a few days later, I called her. She picked up. And we talked about cancer.

"Yep, they got it all. Nope, no chemo. Hold on a second"—coughs—"Sorry, something in my throat. I'm fine. Don't worry about me."

I called her, tentatively, once a month, for the next year. We spoke, but haltingly. I told her I loved her.

And then, a year later, a series of texts on a Friday night from my dad.

"Mom in hospital. They don't know what happened. She's fine."

Everything was not fine. What happened was, in the same bedroom where I'd found her semiconscious at seventeen, my dad found her in the same spot, incoherent. This time, he brought her to the hospital. After a week of texts and prying, I found out she had a stroke.

This was in January 2020, right before COVID lockdown. The stroke was small and impacted the right side of her body. She was able to start physical therapy in person. Again, she wouldn't talk to me on the phone.

"She's worried about the sound of her voice," my dad said.

Then, when COVID hit, she did her stroke exercises in my twin brother's old bedroom, on a recumbent bike paid for by insurance.

"It was a good deal," my dad said.

Months later, she called. And kept calling. Her voice was slightly slurred now, always, but that was something that I had become used to. The slur of a traumatic brain injury is different from the slur of intoxication. But it was familiar.

When I had my child, and went through my own medical emergencies, my mother was there for me, by phone, more than anyone other than my husband. She listened to me. She believed me.

"You're a better mother than I ever was," she said when my daughter turned two. "I'm sorry about everything I did. I'm really so sorry."

I should note that my daughter, Joanna, looks shockingly like my mother. Blond, blue-eyed—same eyes, same nose and mouth. Sometimes I'll watch her playing or eating something and think, *That's Mom.*

"I think Joanna is me reincarnated," my mom told me over the phone.

I didn't get into the metaphysical problems with that statement. What I understood it to mean was I had a child to take care of, who would accept, and welcome, my help.

These conversations released me. When she acknowledged "everything" she did, and apologized, and told me I was a good mother, I was let go from my first job. Plus, I had other logs to keep, such as the ones tracking my daughter's actual logs.

My mom never accepted my help, no matter how hard I tried to force it on her. Al-Anon has a lot to say on this topic. It's not uncommon behavior, either for the child of an alcoholic to try to fix their parent or for the parent to reject the child's attempted help.

But even though my mom wouldn't accept my help, the rigor it took to chart, track, and forecast my mother like a hurricane is a huge part of what made me who I am. The distance I've taken from my parents in the years since is what gave me back so much of myself.

I'm still finding the rest of myself, little by little. That's the work a tryhard can't muscle through. And I still live with a hurricane—but this one dances, and cries, and laughs, and grabs me, and needs me. This little hurricane, a whole life grown from my body, wants, needs, and accepts all the love I have.

Epilogue

That's a substantial portion of our monthly rent.

Danny Blondell, my husband, upon hearing the cost for use of one line of a well-known, and personally beloved, spooktacular song from the middle of the twentieth century, which would have appeared as an epigraph in this exact spot in this book if I hadn't told him what I was planning to pay

Joanna trick-or-treated for the first time this year. She wanted to dress up as a pigeon for Halloween. It turns out, toddler pigeon costumes are hard to come by, because people hate them (pigeons, not toddlers). We settled on a toucan bird suit from the movie *Rio 2*. On Halloween morning Joanna put on her bird costume to "fly" around our apartment.

"I'm going to poop here. And here. And here. Because I'm a pigeon," she said.

We tried to take pictures of her, but she refused, as she proceeded to leave pretend guano all over the apartment. Finally, Danny and I relented and found a video of the Newkirk Plaza B/Q train platform, Joanna's favorite place to spot pigeons. It was only then, while standing in front of the train platform on TV, that she relented to photos. Saying, under her breath, "I'm pooping here. And here. And here."

We picked her up from school to go collect some candy from the neighborhood mansions. It was a clear, unseasonably warm Halloween. Perfect for tricking or treating. The plan was to start near our apartment and walk north, to the locally famous Halloween parade on Albemarle Road. Albemarle is a stretch of the grandest old mansions Brooklyn has to offer. A Tony Award–winning set designer owns one of those mansions, and over the past decade he has outdone himself, Halloween after Halloween. One of the earliest videos we have of Joanna running is her visiting the set designer's Halloween House, on some afternoon in October, darting on the lawn toward a chorus of clanking skeletons hanging from the house's grand porch.

We made our way, via foot and stroller, on the three-quarters-of-a-mile walk to Albemarle, for what we thought would be the end of the baby parade. As we walked we noticed people exiting Lyfts. Young women in tube tops. Men wearing full Santa costumes and holding axes, a genre of costume I still don't understand.

Police began blocking off the streets leading up to the Halloween House. Joanna, so often intimidated by crowds, was transfixed, holding her orange jack-o'-lantern plastic bucket. We passed the Cortelyou train station and saw a group of twenty-something youths exiting the station and also walking north, complete with a trio of mermaids, who were wearing shells on their nipples, with sequined sheaths tucked into their literal thongs.

As my daughter stared and asked about the first thong she'd ever seen ("But where does the butt go?"), it dawned on me: The Halloween House wasn't for babies anymore. Danny and I, for the first time since 2017, were entering the maw of a true-blue party. The secret about the Halloween House had gotten out, you see.

But it was still northward ho.

It seemed that every half-naked reveler was live-streaming their walk. Prior to this inundation, the biggest drama surrounding the Halloween House was that the splendor of the house's decorations had kicked off a Halloween decoration arm's race among the other mansions on Albemarle. Each year, the other houses stepped up their decorations, attempting to catch up to the Halloween House. But, when your basement is full of skeletons from Broadway, rather than Amazon, it's a losing battle.

By the time we got to the Halloween House all the

surrounding streets were blocked off, and helicopters were floating overhead. It was dark by then and hard to see the glory of the original Halloween House.

What wasn't hard to see? The smoke machines, blaring music, and rainbow lights emanating from two of the Halloween House's neighbors.

I took a beta blocker and watched as the young people undulated near all the strollers. At twenty-four I would've taken the train deep into Brooklyn, too, that Thursday night. I would've done a shot of something disgusting, like gin, packed my Young Woman Party Pack (Lexapro, birth control pills, and cigarettes), and gotten to work having a good time. I would've looked at the babies in the strollers, the little blond girl dressed up as a toucan, gotten too close to the stroller, and said, "Hiiiiiii, baby," and squealed to myself or to my friends about how cute all the babies were, while wondering why there were so many babies there.

Dead sober among the undead ax-wielding Santas, I was able to take a step back and see the ghosts of my Brooklyn past and present, standing shoulder to shoulder while the chorus of Michael Jackson's "Smooth Criminal" blasted over a loudspeaker.

I turned to Danny and said, "I think I'm about to have . . ."

"A panic attack?" he said. "Me too."

We retreated from the Halloween House, east on Albemarle, and passed by a less raucous manse. Jonathan Safran Foer's rumored home, to be exact. The poetry board outside said "Candy around the front!" At the front door, two young women in matching white T-shirts stood at a card table twenty feet in front of the house, every room lit up behind them—the homeowners were having a party. If you were a plebe just passing by, you got a full-size candy bar (I held on to Jo's, for posterity). If you were invited to the party? They checked your name off a list or greeted you by name, and allowed you through, into the house. I watched as a man in street clothes and a fedora nodded and passed by the candy sentries, walking up the stairs into the house. When the door opened, I saw a chandelier, beautiful mahogany wood, and a large round entry table with a giant pumpkin display. As quickly as the door opened, it closed.

As I've mentioned, one of the beautiful parts of having a child in a stroller, especially on Halloween, is, as their guardian, you're given social permission to stand by the kid or the stroller and stare. Stare at whatever majesty may or may not be marveling through the child's mind. In this case, the marvel was mine: Were all five bedrooms used as bedrooms, or was there a study? Studies? How much construction would the Landmark rules allow? How much of the original molding stayed with the remodel? Did they have wallpaper in their closets? A mark, I'd learned from a Real Housewife, of a truly decorated home was wallpaper in the walk-ins.

I was definitely in some state of panic disassociation, frozen in my Zillow brain at least, but my fixation on this home, on this idea of stability, grounded me. Slack-jawed while thinking of kitchen fixtures, Danny urged us along. It took me fifteen minutes to realize my hand was so clenched and warm that it had torn the wrapper and melted the candy bar.

My past: a drunken mermaid, with a tail coming out of my thong.

My present: a panicked mom, with a candy bar melting down the arm of my fleece jacket.

My sought-after future: a bright home, with sturdy banisters and original molding.

We fled the scene, down one of the numbered streets, back toward our apartment. Joanna was starting to fade. We couldn't afford her falling asleep in the stroller; the concept of "wake windows"—the period of time a child can be awake before needing to sleep, with the end goal being the elusive sleeping through the night—will never leave my mind, not even when Jo is in her early twenties and hopefully not half naked and surrounded by strollers on Halloween.

Outside of the Halloween Mardi Gras, the mansion owners were sitting outside their homes, on chairs near the street, or on their stoops, kindly handing out candy. Almost every home participated. Some had signs up that said "Candy after 6 o'clock," presumably to tell kids there's no point in showing up for candy until the candymongers (the adults) return home. The neighborhood was alive with the spooky spirit. As we raced home I realized we were about to pass the House—The Gray House.

"Should we do it?" I asked Danny, with a kind of energy

scheme I hadn't felt in years. A bit of the youth rubbed off on me.

"Do . . . what?" he asked, still dazed from Halloween-a-palooza.

"Trick-or-treat at the Gray House," I said.

Danny stopped the stroller and took a look at me, his thirty-seven-year-old wife, wide-eyed, right arm caked in chocolate, sweating in the seventy-five-degree heat.

"I haven't seen you like this for years," he said.

"I'm going to do it."

Danny shrugged and started crossing the street, to the same side as the Gray House.

"NOT THE SAME SIDE. I have to scope it OUT!" I yelled.

I speed-walked—going as fast as I could without bending my knees, which would qualify it as a run—down to the center of the block to see what stance the Gray House owners were taking toward Halloween. Maybe I could glimpse the owner. Or, better yet, maybe they were having a party, their house lit up like a pumpkin.

The Gray House was dark. No lights on at all. And that's when I saw it: someone sitting on their stoop—presumably a resident of the Gray House. This person was sitting outside holding a bowl of candy and wearing a cardboard box on their head. The only openings were small circles for their eyes.

"Let's skip it," I said. "This is too weird."

I've spent years thinking about the Gray House. I've made up an entire backstory for their family, for their lives. I've superimposed a version of myself onto that backstory. I made an entire podcast about that house. I've been personally and professionally known for my obsession over that home. If the owner sitting outside with a cardboard box on their head wasn't a metaphorical message to me that this particular pursuit was over, I don't know what else would be other than owning that actual house.

We got home. Joanna got out of her stroller and dumped out all of her candy onto the kitchen floor, indulging in the innate reflex of a kid organizing their Halloween candy. I washed off my chocolate-coated arm.

"Here, Mommy, you can have this choking hazard," Joanna said. She'd started casually calling Dum-Dums and other things I'd labeled "choking hazards" as choking hazards. "But you have to share with Daddy."

"Okay," I said.

Looking around my apartment—at the washing machine I'd negotiated with my landlord, listening to its peaceful hum; at Joanna's newly erected dollhouse, standing next to a tiny roll of art nouveau wallpaper, yet to be installed by me the next morning; at my daughter pawing peanut butter cups, in complete wonder—I was suddenly pleased. A rare feeling. I wondered if all of this—my family, our home—was a result of my work, or something else. This apartment wasn't, and couldn't, be the Gray House. As I sat with this thought, I stood for a moment, for perhaps the first time, still in my home, with no next step in sight, happy.

Acknowledgments

First, a thank-you to my husband, Danny Blondell. You cared for Joanna every moment I worked on the podcast that sort of became this book. And, again, every time I worked on the Microsoft Word document that actually became this book. I'm so glad you emailed that sad-seeming twenty-four-year-old woman you heard on a podcast in 2011. Thank you for cocreating this very happy-seeming child, Joanna, in 2021.

Secondly, Danielle Svetcov at Levine Greenberg Rostan. Danielle is not only a writer and (in my opinion) the finest agent of all time, she is also perhaps a literal angel. Her work ethic, patience, keen writer's eye, fantastic editing, and kindness and humor in her responses to my countless "Am I crazy?" emails throughout this process pulled this book into being. Thank you for listening to *Shameless Acquisition Target* while riding a stationary bike in your garage back in 2022, and for calling to ask if I had thought about writing a book. I had. And, through your endless help, I did!

Thank you to Elizabeth Mitchell at HarperOne who took a chance on this wily podcast person. Your editorial insight has been invaluable. Thank you, also, to Anna Calame, Kyran Cassidy, and everyone else at HarperOne.

Thank you to Quinn Heraty, my lawyer. You've helped me more than you know. Every time you've suggested that I should consider becoming a lawyer, I've thought, *Is that the biggest hint that I should just become my own lawyer, coming from a lawyer?*

Thanks to Leigh Stein for listening to the *Shameless* podcast and then working with me on the book! *Tryhard Losers* truly did unite.

Thanks to Marina Henke, the brilliant producer on *Shameless Acquisition Target* and the incredibly game research assistant on this book. The sky is the damn limit for you. Thank you for gamely responding to research requests such as: "Can you study all the Girl Scouts' literature from its founding? And also, what happened to all of the meteorologists I loved as a child?" Smart, sharp, down-to-earth, Midwestern (!). What more could I have asked for when working on two largely solitary, and vulnerable, projects?

Thanks, also, to Claire Harvey and Christopher Amaya for your research expertise

Thank you to my friends, and early readers, of this book: Kathy Hua, Mila Mateeva, Jesse Millward, and Jon Stieglitz.

I am forever grateful to Jamilla Ali, Brianna Green, and Stephanie Clarke, three women and educators who have helped Joanna bloom into herself. Jamilla, especially, your boundless heart and care toward developing a community for Joanna continues to go above and beyond. We are so lucky for you all.

Thank you to Gina Anderson and the Ditmas Park Workplace, where I worked on the *Shameless* podcast and this book. Gina, I always appreciated your late-afternoon weekend pep talks and your commitment to Ditmas Park.

Thank you to Mina McAllister and Kate Soloff. Making mother friends was a real struggle for me, as I was mainly friends with my computer while on the toil at work. You two, and the group chat, gave me a lot of hope in many dark times.

Thank you to Sabina Galli, who accepted me as a client more than ten years ago, even though I spent our entire first session sobbing. You've changed my life.

I'm about to thank my family, which is why I'm thanking you here, Karen Shimmin, the closest thing to a biological sister I'll ever have. Can you believe that it's been more than twenty years since we met? You're a magnificent writer, mother, business owner, and a true friend.

Thank you to Lilly and Martin, Joanna and Danny's biggest fans and supporters. Thank you, also, to Helene, Samantha, David, Z, Jon, Andrew, Christine, and Iona. Brian, I miss you.

It's tricky to write (and *to read, thank YOU*) a book framed by childhood trauma. Thank you to my parents for being okay with me telling my story. My parents are miraculous people who have shown that growth and change is possible. And with that, for all three of us, came forgiveness, acceptance, and, as ever, love.